is a
Four-Letter Word

---

by
RANDALL STEWART

with
CINDY STEWART

Cheryl & Denise,
To your Success!
Randall & Cindy

TRAFFORD
USA • Canada • UK • Ireland

© Copyright 2006 Randall Stewart.
All rights reserved. No part of this publication may be reproduced, stored in a retrieval system, or transmitted, in any form or by any means, electronic, mechanical, photocopying, recording, or otherwise, without the written prior permission of the author.

Note for Librarians: A cataloguing record for this book is available from Library and Archives Canada at www.collectionscanada.ca/amicus/index-e.html
ISBN 1-4120-9998-6

Printed in Victoria, BC, Canada. Printed on paper with minimum 30% recycled fibre.
Trafford's print shop runs on "green energy" from solar, wind and other environmentally-friendly power sources.

Offices in Canada, USA, Ireland and UK

Book sales for North America and international:
Trafford Publishing, 6E–2333 Government St.,
Victoria, BC V8T 4P4 CANADA
phone 250 383 6864 (toll-free 1 888 232 4444)
fax 250 383 6804; email to orders@trafford.com

Book sales in Europe:
Trafford Publishing (UK) Limited, 9 Park End Street, 2nd Floor
Oxford, UK OX1 1HH UNITED KINGDOM
phone 44 (0)1865 722 113 (local rate 0845 230 9601)
facsimile 44 (0)1865 722 868; info.uk@trafford.com

Order online at:
trafford.com/06-1755

10 9 8 7 6 5 4 3 2

ACKNOWLEDGEMENTS

Randall:

I am forever grateful to my parents, Marianne and Joseph, for your unconditional love, on-going support and patience with me as I have grown and matured.

Thank you to my dear friend, Patrick Erwert, whose upbeat positive attitude, competitive spirit and priceless friendship have been a true blessing to me. Many thanks to Céline Godin, for your joie de vivre, continuing support and of course your incredible patience in putting up with Patrick and me.

To Jean and Marilyn Savoie, thank you for your entrepreneurial spirit, your kind-heartedness and believing in us.

Cindy:

A big thank you to my dear friend, Karen Nordyke, who has not only been a good listener, but she has always been honest and frank with me. Thank you for believing in me and being such a gracious giver.

To my lifelong friend, Gerry Douglas, thank you for your heartfelt sincerity, positive attitude and belief in my potential.

Together:

We would like to thank our total success publishing team that has been instrumental in pulling everything together to produce this guide, which we hope will transform the lives of all that embark on their own total success journey. Many thanks to an awesome team at Trafford Publishing, to our illustrator and cover designer, Ken Faulks, and to our photographer, Chris Cornett, who all have been a joy and pleasure to work with.

We are deeply grateful to Craig and Donna Tufts for your inspiration, unconditional love and on-going spiritual support.

Another heartfelt thank you goes out to all the staff at Stores Online for allowing us to see the unlimited opportunities to market our knowledge, our passions and our dreams of creating a better world. Finally, we would like to thank everyone at the Institute for Financial Learning for opening our eyes and minds to the countless abundance at our fingertips.

TABLE OF CONTENTS

Introduction   7
     What is success?
     How is this guide organized?
     Why fifty days?
     How do I get the most out of this guide?

Day One   **Where Am I At In My Life?**   12
     My wants and desires
     My dreams
     My values
     My vision
     Goal setting

Day Two   **My Spiritual Life**   25
     Discovering my purpose
     Adding value to other people's lives
     Reaching my maximum potential
     The power of prayer
     Formulating my top three spiritual goals
     Cindy's success tips & suggestions

Day Three   **My Relationships**   41
     It all starts with effective communication
     Serving others
     Connecting with my family
     Strengthening my marriage
     Building lasting friendships
     Resolving relational problems
     Attracting ideal people
     Formulating my top three relationship goals
     Cindy's success tips & suggestions

Day Four   **Expanding My Mind**   58
     Learning how to learn
     Ten tips to improving your mental capacity

Reading the right way
Reading comprehension and remembering longer
Formulating my top three learning goals
Cindy's success tips & suggestions

Day Five   **My Physical Well-being**   **70**

Basic fitness principles
Nutrition
Achieving optimal health
Formulating my top three physical well-being goals
Cindy's success tips & suggestions

Day Six   **My Emotional Development**   **88**

My beliefs influence my attitudes
My action steps
Formulating my top three emotional development goals
Cindy's success tips & suggestions

Day Seven   **My Finances & Career**   **105**

What is financial freedom?
Two key attitudes to becoming financially free
My money management strategies
How do I become financially free?
Promoting my value
Finding the right investment plan
Cindy's success tips & suggestions

Day Eight   **Piecing It All Together Where am I at?**   **123**

Selecting my top six goals
What about my total success team?
Attracting my first mentor
My most powerful ally – my journal

Daily Journal   132
Where Do I Go From Here?   175
About the authors   177

Introduction

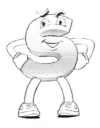

"Success is a four-letter word."

Congratulations!

You have taken the first step to creating more abundance, prosperity and joy in your life by picking up this step-by-step guide. By investing in this resource, you have invested in yourself.

Reading this book will assist you in becoming more successful in many aspects of your life. But in order for permanent positive change to occur, you must move beyond just reading and <u>commit to doing</u>. If you have a burning desire to make a difference in your life, as well as in the lives of individuals you touch, then make a real commitment by following the suggested learning strategies. Be an active learner. Most people reading books or taking seminars don't take the time to implement what they have learned to create permanent change. Be different! Take the initiative now and commit to a fifty-day transformation process that will move you in the direction of becoming more successful.

We ask that you reserve critical judgment of this guide for at least one month. Success is a learned skill. Allow yourself the time to develop and improve. Keep an open mind to the various possibilities for growth by being actively engaged in the learning process. No resource or teaching method is right for everyone. Rather than debating with yourself as to whether the various strategies presented in this guide will work for you, embark on a new, exciting journey and focus on creating positive change in all aspects of your life. Use this guide as a continuous work-in-progress that will act as the catalyst to inspire you to take action and grow to your full potential.

> If we value independence, if we are disturbed by the growing conformity of knowledge, of values, of attitudes, which our present system induces, then we may wish to set up conditions of learning which make for uniqueness, for self-direction, and for self-initiated learning.
>
> **Carl Rogers**

WHAT IS SUCCESS?

Earl Nightingale likes to say "success is the progressive realization of a worthy goal." According to this definition, success is not the achievement of a goal, but a journey toward the fulfillment of a personal or moral value or ideal.

This book will guide you through the process of identifying your dreams, desires and values in order to develop a vision and clear, concise goals in the six focus areas for "Total Success," namely:

- My Spiritual Life: *Leaving a Legacy*
- My Relationships: *Loving*
- Expanding My Mind: *Learning*
- My Physical Well-being: *Living*
- My Emotional Development: *Laughing*
- My Finances and Career: *Looking for Opportunities*

To be truly successful, both Cindy and I believe that one should strive to:

Leave both an earthly and eternal *Legacy*, founded in unconditional *Love*, based on a desire to *Learn* continuously, with the conviction to *Live* our lives to the fullest. Successful individuals have the ability to *Laugh* and take pleasure in life, and develop the skills to *Look* for opportunities to *Leverage* both time and financial resources for the betterment of mankind.

Successful individuals consistently display a number of key elements, namely:

1. Vision: moving towards a specific dream and set of goals
2. Passion: being motivated, energized and inspired by one's vision
3. Focus: committing one's time, energy and resources to specific priorities
4. Drive: taking consistent purposeful action
5. Strategic plan: following a clear written process and realistic time-line
6. Support: involving key individuals who have special talents or abilities
7. Courage: expanding one's knowledge and being willing to try new challenges
8. Flexibility: being open to exploring alternatives or new opportunities
9. Balance: managing one's spiritual, mental, physical and emotional health
10. Positive nature: choosing to have a constructive growth-oriented attitude

11. Sharing: giving of one's time, energy and resources for others
12. Gratitude: being appreciative of the blessings and benefits one has received.

HOW IS THIS GUIDE ORGANIZED?

Research indicates that people learn better when several senses are involved in learning concepts and committing them to long-term memory. People prefer different learning styles or modalities. Many of us can recognize that we are visual, auditory or tactile learners. How do you prefer receiving information? By seeing it? Listening to it? Or through actions and feeling it? Approximately seventy-five percent of us are visual learners. The activities designed around meeting the learning needs of these individuals come in the form of diagrams, charts, tables, graphic organizers and cartoons. Between fifteen and twenty percent of us learn best by listening. We encourage you to use the declarations presented in the guide, discuss concepts and ideas with others or read sections aloud. Primarily tactile or kinaesthetic learners should take notes, draw, write or make movement and actions their focus. Since most of us have strengths in more than one learning modality, this guide has incorporated a number of different learning styles throughout to better meet your needs as a learner.

Each letter in the word SUCCESS represents a specific strategy that will optimize your learning. The learning process in each chapter is organized based on the following:

S Self-awareness: what related prior knowledge do you have?

U Understanding: making connections to what you know.

C Content: developing main ideas and key concepts.

C Concept attainment: learning new concepts.

E Engaging: taking specific action steps to apply your knowledge.

S Success tips: various suggestions and strategies to implement.

S Suggested resources: exploring future possibilities.

WHY FIFTY DAYS?

You may be asking yourself, why fifty days? In order for physiological adaptations to take place in the body or mind, change or adaptation needs to occur over time. As the body is presented with new stimuli, its response is to adapt to the changes by growing. Significant physical changes to our bodies may occur in as little as one month, whereas emotional and attitudinal changes may require several months. Given a fifty-day time period, you will be able to realistically monitor, measure and maintain your progress and focus.

HOW DO I GET THE MOST OUT OF THIS GUIDE?

Our primary goal is to provide you with the essential concepts required for you to begin your total success journey, coupled with some of the most effective learning strategies to bring about meaningful, long-term change.

We recommend that you work through the first seven chapters over a one-week period. This will enable you to better assimilate the information presented, as well as take the time necessary for self-awareness and planning.

Please take the time to work through all of the learning strategies presented. Focus on developing your potential in all six total success areas. To experience true success, in all its senses, you need a rich, meaningful balance between your spiritual life, your relationships with family, friends and colleagues, your understanding of the world around you, your physical and mental health, and your finances and career.

Our hope and desire is that your total success journey will enable you to eventually reach your full potential and find your life purpose in adding value to other people's lives. We encourage you to continue being an active, lifelong learner. Seek out the wealth of knowledge and expertise offered by all the "success gurus" mentioned in this guide.

"Getting in touch with your true self will unleash the incredible potential that is within you now."

INTRODUCTION

Are you ready? Now is the time to make your fifty-day commitment.

My Commitment to Total Success in fifty days or less

From this day forth, I, _____, commit myself to:

- learning how to become successful in all aspects of my life
- embarking on a journey to discover my dreams, passions and talents
- discovering my purpose in life
- growing to reach my full potential
- adding value to other people's lives

I will focus on opportunities to grow, rather than obstacles.

I will expand my comfort zone and act in spite of fear, uncertainty and inconvenience.

I will do whatever it takes to become more and more successful.

Signature: _____   Date:_____

You will encounter many distractions and many temptations to put your goal aside: The security of a job, a wife who wants kids, whatever. But if you hang in there, always following your vision, I have no doubt you will succeed.

Larry Flynt

Day One

Where am I at in my life?

What do I really know about myself?

What are my real desires and hopes?

What do I truly value in life?

These and other questions are the focal point of this chapter so that you may gain a better understanding as to who you are and what your convictions are. Your dreams are shaped by your values and created from your wants and core desires. Each of these fundamental components provides you with the essential building blocks for creating your total success plan.

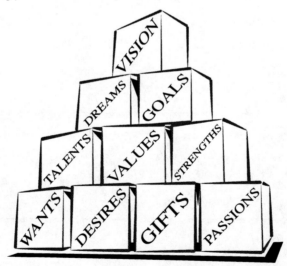

We suggest that you set aside a block of time, such as a couple of hours, away from the distractions of the office, friends or family, in order to work through the following material as honestly as you can.

WHERE AM I AT IN MY LIFE?

MY WANTS AND DESIRES

Using the space below, write down what you want to BE, DO or HAVE:

1. _____

2. _____

3. _____

4. _____

5. _____

Everyone knows what he or she wants or desires, but many of us are simply afraid to admit it. By admitting that you have certain wants or desires, you must also take ownership of the fact that you don't have what you want in your life. Rather than make excuses or ignore these wants, align your desires with what God would want for you. What you think you want in life as seen from the limited perspective of your conscious mind may not be in alignment with your life purpose or mission. When your core desire is in alignment with God's desire for you and the world, a whole universe of opportunities and abundance opens up to you.

Mother Teresa wrote, "We spend a great deal of time telling God what we think should be done, and not enough time waiting in the stillness for God to tell us what to do."

Your task now is to state your intention as to what you really want in life. Ask simply and honestly for what your heart desires without placing limitations as to a specific person, place or time for your desire to be fulfilled.

Using the space below, write down what your heart is telling you about what you really want to BE, DO or HAVE:

1. _____

2. _____

3. _____

4. _____

5. _____

MY DREAMS

George Bernard Shaw once said, "You see things and say Why? but I dream things that never were and I say Why not?" Your next step in your total success journey is to begin the process of identifying your dreams. Once you have identified your dreams, we will help you clarify and fine-tune them so that you will know what direction to take and what purpose you are moving towards.

Try to list at least six of your current dreams right now. Start each statement with an action verb. Choose from the following list, or use your own specific action words.

attain	create	develop	design	aid
complete	accomplish	fulfill	implement	maintain
learn	improve	increase	add	encourage
make	achieve	contribute	promote	advise
retire	reduce	train	realize	free
guide	write	build	support	strengthen

1. _____
2. _____
3. _____
4. _____
5. _____
6. _____
7. _____
8. _____
9. _____
10. _____

Our dreams start us on our success journey. They focus our energy and time in moving down a specific,

Where Am I At In My Life?

chosen path. In doing so, we set priorities in the present in order to move towards realizing what is down that inevitable path into the future. Dreams allow us to grow to our full potential. They add value and meaning to our lives. Your dream coupled with a positive attitude presents you with countless possibilities and unlimited potential.

Keep in mind that in order to discover and develop your dreams you will need to:

- be clear about your intentions
- allow your feelings and emotions to embody your dreams
- focus on realizing your dream, no matter what
- allow time for your dreams to grow and develop
- share your dreams with others.

Take your time and fill in the following information, which will be used to shape your dreams. Give some thought as to where you are right now and how far you are from realizing your dreams.

If I could be anything I wanted, what would I become? Why?

_____

_____

_____

_____

_____

_____

"You live in a world of incredible opportunities, unlimited abundance and endless creativity. What may seem impossible to you today, could be your reality tomorrow."

Success is a Four-Letter Word

What are my greatest talents?

What are the natural endowments or innate abilities people say I excel?

In the following table, take the time to reflect on each of the statements. Place a check mark next to the talents that you consistently display. Should you identify other talents unique to you, add them at the bottom of the table.

Please note that the talents have been loosely grouped into six areas. These groupings are meant to guide you later in developing your total success plan.

Spiritual		I show empathy towards others.
		I possess strong beliefs.
		I feel strongly connected with everyone.
		I work towards harmony and agreement.
		I enjoy building close relationships.
Relationships		I enjoy meeting and getting to know new people.
		I focus on an individual's unique qualities.
		I am flexible.
		I like to take charge.
		I enjoy developing the potential in others.
		I include people and make them feel welcome.
Educational/mental		I am an active learner.
		I have an inquisitive mind.
		I am a dreamer and a visionary.
		I like to think and stretch my mental capacity.
		I have creative ideas.
Physical/health		I thrive on competition and performance.
		I focus on maximizing my potential.
Attitude/emotional		I have a positive attitude and happy disposition.
		I love to achieve and succeed.
		I am careful and deliberate.
		I am disciplined in what I do.
		I take responsibility for my commitments.
Financial/career		I have an analytical mind.
		I like to organize and arrange things.
		I am able to focus and be efficient.

Where Am I At In My Life?

		I love to solve problems and enjoy fixing things.
		I want to be significant in the eyes of others.

What are my greatest character traits? What is it about my personality that is a desirable attribute? Place a check mark next to the traits that you display consistently.

accepting		devout		instinctive		polite	
admirable		easygoing		intellectual		practical	
adventurous		efficient		kind		prepared	
affectionate		energetic		knowledgeable		proud	
ambitious		enthusiastic		loving		punctual	
appreciative		faithful		mature		qualified	
artistic		flexible		meticulous		rational	
calm		friendly		moral		reasonable	
cautious		funny		musical		reserved	
cheerful		generous		observant		responsible	
competent		grateful		open		selfless	
competitive		healthy		optimistic		skillful	
conscientious		helpful		orderly		steadfast	
considerate		honest		passionate		tactful	
cooperative		humble		patient		trustworthy	
creative		independent		persistent		understanding	
determined		inquisitive		pleasant		youthful	

How can I create opportunities or free up my time and resources that will enable me to better realize my dreams?

1. _____

2. _____

3. _____

4. _____

5. _____

What specific obstacles that I can control lie in my way of realizing my dreams?

What will I have to overcome in order to achieve my dreams?

1. _____

2. _____

3. _____

4. _____

5. _____

Of the following factors, what will I have to specifically give up or sacrifice in order to accomplish my dreams?

Time: _____

Money/assets: _____

Relationships: _____

Present job/career: _____

Comfort/luxuries: _____

Other options: _____

"Who could I enlist the help of to support my endeavours? "

"Who would be a good candidate for my total success team?"

WHERE AM I AT IN MY LIFE?

MY VALUES

What do you value in your personal life? in your relationships?

Are your values aligned with your desires?

A value is a principle regarded as being worthwhile or desirable. It is a principle that governs your actions, no matter what may transpire. Values are key building blocks in creating a strong foundation for one's life. They provide us with the inspiration that influences our day-to-day choices. We create our vision based on our values and dreams. The more committed we are to our values, the easier it becomes to create our vision and ultimately to determine our mission or purpose in life.

In order to build upon developing your own vision statement, you first need to identify the values that you deem important. The following Venn diagram has loosely grouped a number of key values into the six areas for total success. Rank each of the values in importance on a scale of one to five, with 1 being least important, three being neutral in importance, and 5 being the most important. Should you identify other values of importance to you, add them to the centre of the diagram.

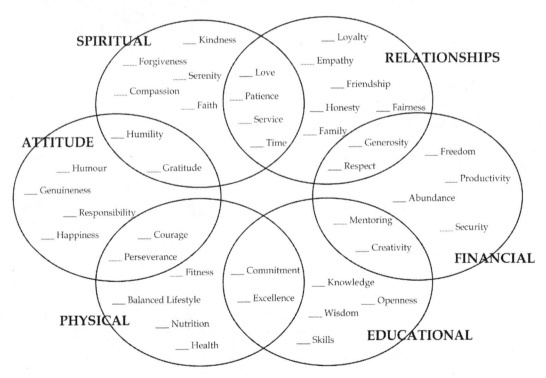

Unconditional, no-strings-attached love is the most important value to hold closest to your heart if you would like to be aligned with God's ultimate plan for your life. Besides the fundamental value of showing unconditional love to all, we also need to consider other essential values vital to attracting abundance and prosperity into our lives and the lives that we touch. Based on the values loosely associated with each of the six total success areas, we would like to suggest that the following values are worthy of consideration and focus:

- *Integrity:* being committed to living and acting truthfully
- *Gratitude:* being in a constant state of appreciation and thankfulness
- *Generosity:* sharing and giving freely of your material wealth or your time
- *Commitment:* being fully engaged in something you have pledged to do
- *Loyalty:* being faithful to others, to organizations or to causes
- *Compassion:* being sympathetic and supportive of others' distress
- *Responsibility:* being accountable for your behaviour or actions.

Congratulations! You have taken another important step to being closer to realizing your dreams and establishing your vision, which will attract more abundance, prosperity and joy into your life.

MY VISION

Your vision is the specific image you establish in your mind of where you want to go in life. A dream will become a vision when we test it, truly commit to it, and can make it real and do something with it. While many of us may hold the same dreams in life, visions are not all the same. Creating and working towards your vision means that you need to find a higher purpose for your dreams. To guide you in this process, we will take a moment to identify and integrate your passions, motivations and spiritual gifts into a preliminary vision statement.

What are my passions? What are the things I love to do so much that I would gladly do them for free?

1. _____
2. _____
3. _____
4. _____

Where Am I At In My Life?

What factors in my life motivate me in my:

spiritual life? _____

family life? _____

community involvement? _____

intellectual growth? _____

health and fitness? _____

emotional well-being? _____

finances and career? _____

A big part of your life will be discovering what your God-given talents are. What do you think are your spiritual gifts, those special God-empowered abilities for serving him through others? Your spiritual gifts are almost always confirmed by others and what they see in you. Ask those close to you for their candid opinion.

1. _____

2. _____

3. _____

4. _____

5. _____

At the end of my earthly life:

What are the top three life lessons I will have learned? Briefly state why.

1. _____
   _____

2. _____
   _____

3. _____
   _____

What one-sentence inscription would I like written on my tombstone to reflect who I really was during my life?

_____

_____

Spend a few minutes reviewing all the information you have written so far in your self-awareness and self-evaluation process. Taking into consideration the key ideas and elements that you have identified, write a draft of your vision statement that reflects your deepest values, talents and passions for adding value to other people's lives. Your statement should be inspirational and ambitious, yet realistic. Write your draft in the present tense using action verbs.

_____

_____

_____

_____

GOAL-SETTING

Your dreams and vision determine the goals you need in order to act on and create the results that bring you success. In other words, your goals are the accomplishments that you plan to complete in order to realize your dreams and fulfill your life purpose.

What do goals provide you with? Why set goals?

- Goals motivate and energize you.
- Goals guide your actions, showing you what to do next.
- Goals focus your attention on what needs to be done.
- Goals keep you on your path towards total success.
- Goals monitor your progress along your total success journey.
- Goals give you greater clarity as to your sense of purpose.

Success manifests itself in the progressive and timely achievement of your goals.

In the following chapters, we will use these guidelines to help you develop your specific goals for each of the six focus areas for total success.

Your goals should be:

Written

The writing process helps to clarify your objectives. It also is a visual commitment that makes you more accountable for your actions and behaviours. State your goals as single, concise sentences and use specific action verbs.

Specific

With increased clarity comes an increased opportunity. Focus on how you can become more specific in writing each goal in terms of events and behaviours. You want to be absolutely clear about what you intend to do to quickly identify, locate, create and implement the use of necessary resources for achieving each goal.

Personal

Each goal must be yours, not somebody else's, such as your boss's, spouse's or best friend's. Don't worry about what everyone else thinks. Focus on what you would like to accomplish.

Meaningful

Here are some focus questions that may guide your goal creation process. Ask yourself: "What is important to me? Why follow this specific goal? What are the rewards and benefits?"

Flexible

Your goals should not be written in stone. You should have the freedom to deviate slightly from your course if circumstances provide you with a beneficial opportunity to pursue.

Measurable

Ask yourself, "How will I know that I am achieving my goals?" You need to create accountability for your actions and progress. Express each goal in terms that allow it to be measured in progressive steps or tasks.

Challenging

Your goals should be exciting enough to force you out of your comfort zone. Learning and your ability to succeed occur only when you are exploring something new.

Realistic

As you compose your goals, ask yourself, "Is each goal within my power to achieve or accomplish? Are my goals believable?"

Time-sensitive

A deadline forces you to change your mindset from simply dreaming to realizing. When you assign each goal a time limit, try to be realistic about how long it will take to achieve it. A good rule-of-thumb is to double the time you initially think it will take.

Aligned with your positive values

When you create harmony between your fundamental beliefs and your life direction, you attract more abundance and prosperity into your life.

Supported

Enlist the help of others. Together, you may be able to work in unity towards a common goal, life direction or good. Keep in mind that you should never sacrifice your relationships over the long run for any goal.

Well-balanced

To truly be successful as a holistic being, you need to develop goals in the many facets or aspects of your life. Creating that harmony and balance will bring you that much closer to achieving total success in your life.

Where do we go from here with all this information?

Your focus in the next chapter will be to use your preliminary information about your core desires, values and dreams in order to prepare your mission or life purpose statement. Once you have written your life purpose statement, you will be able to focus on developing specific goals, which will be aligned with your life purpose for each of the six areas of your total success plan.

Day Two My spiritual life

Why am I here?

What is my duty or responsibility to society?

How could I better serve God and my fellow man?

In the last chapter, we identified many factors that influence and shape who we are and how we may serve others. The combination of our spiritual gifts, passions, abilities, personality traits and experiences in life determines how successful we become. You have taken the initial steps to discovering how these factors influence your dreams, your vision and ultimately your life purpose.

Our universe has an intelligent design. We did not show up on Earth by chance. That intelligent design was shaped through God's creation and as a result we have been created in God's image. Ask yourself, "Why was I created?" In truth, you came into this life with a specific life purpose or mission. Without a life purpose, there is emptiness in our reason for being. In essence, we are spiritual beings having an earthly experience, not human beings having a spiritual experience. Our greatest joy is discovering that our mission in life is based on the unique combination of talents, gifts, passions and experiences that we have. It is your duty and responsibility to succeed and contribute to society and others' lives. By following God's intentions and desires for you, you will be unstoppable in your journey towards total success.

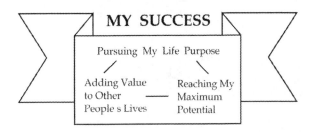

Here are some of the benefits of aligning your goals with God's plan for you:

- It gives meaning and hope to your earthly life.
- It simplifies your life in being able to discern between what you do and don't do.
- It focuses your effort and energy on what is important.
- It motivates you in having a clear purpose.
- It creates a passion and joy for living your life to the fullest.
- It prepares you for eternity.

My Spiritual Life

DISCOVERING MY PURPOSE

What are you grateful for? Fill in the table below with those specific relationships, experiences and situations that have entered your life.

	In my spiritual life I am grateful for:
	In my relationships I am grateful for:
	In expanding my mind I am grateful for:
	In my physical well-being I am grateful for:
	In my emotional development I am grateful for:
	In my finances and career I am grateful for:

It is sad to say that the vast majority of people on Earth live in a state of poverty, oppression or severe hardship compared to what our North American culture has to offer. When you take a moment to compare your life to those in third world countries, you quickly see that you are living an abundant life. Realizing this, take a moment to acknowledge and be sincerely grateful for those relationships, experiences or situations that have been true blessings for you. By feeling truly grateful for the abundance in your life right now, you open yourself up to attracting more abundance.

We come from a divine source that is eternal, unlimited, inclusive and loving. To find your life purpose, let go of having to do it your way, and let God infuse your inner spirit with his life purpose for you. The following exercise may help to gently nudge you in that direction. Have your spouse, a close family member, a dear friend or a mentor either jot down on paper or record on a cassette your answers to this simple question: "What is God's destiny for you?" Have your partner keep repeating the question and recording your different responses for a period of five minutes. Keep your mind completely open to any possibilities. What transpires may surprise you. Hopefully, by opening up and letting go, you will arrive at your heart's desire. When you reflect on what has been said, you may be in a better position to develop your life purpose statement.

My life purpose statement

Will your life purpose statement answer these three fundamental questions?

- Am I following my calling?
- Am I making a difference?
- Am I attracting success into my life?

Base your statement of purpose on:

1. Your preliminary vision statement, your most important dreams, your values and how you could use your natural abilities.
2. What you intend on being and doing while you are going in that direction.
3. A single, concise, powerful statement that focuses your daily activities.
4. Your personal definition of success.
5. How you will add value to your life and others.

Here are a couple of examples of life purpose statements:

My life purpose is to serve my fellow man with my medical skills, share my love and talents with all the lives I touch, lead my family and others to serve God in my community and be a positive role model to all.

My life purpose is to worship God with my heart, strive to be like him in character, serve him with my gifts, engage in fellowship with my church community and share my life message with others through my teaching.

Do your best to write your mission statement. Plan to make changes to your statement as you discover more about yourself and grow towards your full potential.

My life purpose is to: _____

_____

_____

_____

_____

Write or type up your statement and then either post it in a place where you would see it over the next fifty days or carry it with you in your pocket. By doing so, you will be subtly reminding yourself of your intentions.

ADDING VALUE TO OTHER PEOPLE'S LIVES

How could I add value to other people's lives?

Your accomplishments during your life are not the true measure of your success on Earth, but rather what you have done for others. Be resolved to make a positive difference in other people's lives.

In order to add value to others' lives, you need to:

- Value people. Accept individuals for who they are, treating them with dignity and respect. Your goal is to motivate individuals, not to manipulate them.
- Know and relate to what others value. Listen and pay attention to both their words and their feelings.
- Make yourself more valuable. Become an active, continuous learner.

Begin by thinking more like a servant in all your relationships, rather than a master. Your focus will shift to doing more for others as opposed to getting what you can from others. You will shift from being self-centred to being selfless and self-giving. You will also look at life everywhere on this planet as being your responsibility to maintain, enhance and preserve for future generations. You will begin to act as a steward of this planet rather than as an owner.

Another important aspect of your mission in life is sharing your life message with others. Your life lessons may be a valuable source of inspiration for others. Make a point of allowing others to learn from your experiences. Be a source of motivation and hope for those who are less fortunate than you.

We are both spiritual and human "beings," not human "doings." When God sees you being in touch with your life purpose of adding value to other people's lives, he will surely provide you with unlimited riches. Those riches may not be in the material wealth sense of the word, but rather those riches found through meaningful relationships or the incredible satisfaction of creating positive change and making a significant difference in this world. Are you following your calling? Are you making a difference?

An important part of your development as a spiritual being is the act of giving from the heart. As you give from the heart without expecting anything in return, you open yourself up to receiving more of God's grace. You will feel more generous. You will feel better about yourself. You will have a more successful life. Giving can be broken down into four interrelated areas, namely:

Giving of your time

Your time on this Earth is finite or limited. One of your greatest gifts to someone is spending quality time helping him or her reach their full potential as human beings.

List three things that you could do to better manage your time so that you can give more of yourself:

1. _____

2. _____

3. _____

Giving of your energy

Your spiritual energy shows up in your passion, commitment and integrity for those deeply held values that move you beyond your own self-interests to those of others. How you manage your energy affects your performance. It comes down to a question of choice. Some choices energize us, while others create barriers. We all have certain barriers that get in the way of harnessing our full energy potential and of using the energy available for improving the quality of life for others. Some of those common barriers are found in being pessimistic, impatient, inflexible or critical. In order for your spiritual energy to be better aligned with your life purpose, it is essential that you shift your energy from negative to positive and from self to others.

Giving of your God-given talents

The best way for you to truly discover your spiritual gifts is to start serving in a number of different areas of service. In doing so, you increase the likelihood of revealing what you are good at. Keep experimenting with different areas of service no matter what age you are. You may discover hidden talents well into your seventies or eighties. You will never know what you are good at until you try.

List three things that you could do in your immediate work environment that would give more of yourself to helping your colleagues reach their full potential:

1. _____
2. _____
3. _____

Giving of your material resources

We have all heard the expression that whoever sows generously will reap generously. Giving a portion of your financial blessings to help those less fortunate than you is a true measure of your success as a human being. Get into the habit of setting aside ten percent of your income to help others, whether it is at your local place of worship, a philanthropic cause, or even by creating jobs for others. Give even when you don't have. Don't wait until you are financially successful or out of debt. Get into the habit of giving regularly.

List three things that you could change today to increase your level of financial giving:

1. _____
2. _____
3. _____

Be resolved to make a positive difference in the lives of those that you touch. When you strive to reach a point of harmony and balance between all six areas for achieving total success, you are in a better position to impact other people's lives. It is your passion for your vision coupled with the discipline required to follow your mission that is guided by your moral conscience, which will inspire others.

REACHING MY MAXIMUM POTENTIAL

In order to live your life purpose, you should always keep in mind the balance that should exist between each of the developmental areas for total success.

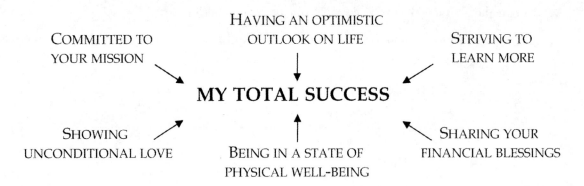

Do you believe in your potential?

A key component to success is being able to grow towards reaching your maximum potential. God has given us unique talents and the potential to use them. What we do with our talents and potential is our way of honoring him.

To work towards reaching your full potential, keep these points in mind:

1. Reaching your potential requires focus on your goals, which means that you will need to concentrate on those elements that benefit your growth and sacrifice those factors that take you away from achieving your full potential. Give your energy and your time only to those elements that draw you closer to your life purpose.

2. Concentrate your efforts on continuously learning and growing for the better. To improve the quality of your life and those around you, improve yourself.

3. Forget what has transpired in the past and focus on what you need to do for reaching your full potential. We cannot change the past. Rather, look for the lessons that may be learned from your past experiences.

4. Talk is cheap. Start working towards developing your full potential today. Commit to your self-development, which will bring you closer to realizing your life purpose.

5. Keep challenging and pushing your preconceived boundaries or "comfort zone." True growth occurs only when you step out of your set and familiar ways and dare yourself to achieve and improve. Model growth and a willingness to change and move out of your comfort zone.

6. Enjoy and celebrate your accomplishments and successes. Reward yourself from time to time, such as going out to dinner in a fancy restaurant or spending an hour at a spa.

7. Create a positive growth environment for you and those with whom you work or live. Surround yourself with people from whom you can learn. Develop an affirming, supportive and caring demeanour.

THE POWER OF PRAYER

Our physical world is made up of atoms that are in a constant state of resonating vibrations of energy. Our interaction with the universe is through the flow of energy and information, which is alive as thought. Your thoughts are energy and have the power to transform. If you are clear about your intentions, the energy moves in one direction towards manifesting your desires. If you are unclear about your desires, the energy of your thoughts scatters, losing its impact. If you are obsessed with or insistent about having your desires fulfilled, your energy will surely meet with resistance. When you desire something, yet are fine with not receiving it, then you are more likely to attract it into your life. The thought of giving, the thought of blessing and the act of prayer have the power to affect others when they are grounded in the deep, heart-felt emotion of faith. When what you desire is clear and aligned with God, that intention is on its way to being manifested in your life. When you learn to let go and trust in God, you open yourself up to attracting more abundance and prosperity into your life.

Prayer is your spiritual communication with God through thought or word. One powerful use of prayer is in formulating specific requests for help from God. Your prayer request for help in achieving an optimal outcome needs to be clear. It also needs to take into account the effect on your lifestyle should your request be granted. Many individuals focus on praying for specific results to occur, yet fail to consider the possible consequences involved should their prayers be answered. It is therefore imperative that you take a moment to clearly formulate your specific prayer requests and carefully consider how they may affect your lifestyle. There are countless possibilities. Aligning your prayer request with your desired impact on your preferred lifestyle while taking into consideration what God's intentions are for your life, becomes the challenge. You can only do your best in trying to bring all the necessary elements together and leave it up to God to allow your intentions to manifest themselves.

Keep in mind these seven steps for formulating your prayer requests:

1. Assess the type of help that you need. Should you have several prayer requests, prioritize them by importance and potential impact on your life.

2. Begin to develop clarity for your request based on the answers to the following questions:

    - Is my prayer request in line with my mission?

- Will I be adding value to other people's lives?
- Is my request success-oriented in helping me reach my full potential?
- What is standing in the way of my request and ultimately my success?

3. Determine which lifestyle components matter the most to you. How would my granted request impact:
   - my work hours or working conditions?
   - the kind of people entering my life?
   - my living conditions?
   - my relationships?
   - my leisure time and activities?

4. Formulate your prayer request.

Take your time in formulating your prayer request. Write a rough draft of your request, and then set it aside overnight. In doing so, your subconscious mind will be able to clarify and fine-tune your request. You may even want to consider using a word processor to help facilitate the editing process and keep track of your prayer requests. The next day, read over your initial draft and edit it as you see fit. Repeat this process as often as you feel is needed over the next few days. Do not rush this process. Some requests may require several weeks to formulate.

Here are some tips to consider in formulating your prayer requests:

- Be precise about what you want.
- Leave your possible response options open-ended.
- Be optimistic, yet realistic.
- Briefly explain why you would like something.
- Ask for an appropriate sign to help you determine if your request has been granted.
- Begin by using a simple template to guide you in the writing process.

An example of one follows:

Dear God,

I would like help with finding a specific area in my local community where I could use my God-given talents to add value to the lives of those people who are less fortunate than I am.

(Write a short summary statement or overview of what you would like help with.)

Please bless me by allowing those people, ideas, resources or opportunities to enter into my life so that I can:

1. *find the right situation where my talents and skills will be of value to others either before or after my job*
2. *attract the right people to join me in achieving my goals, and help them achieve their goals, while we are all having a lot of fun*
3. *gain greater satisfaction for accomplishing good in my neighbourhood.*

Although I have good intentions of helping others, I have yet to find a place in my local community where I may serve the needs of others and help change their lives for the better.

(List the specific thing(s) with which you would like help. Start each statement with an action verb. Include details as appropriate. Finish each statement with your reason why you would like it.)

I ask that you give me this or something better as I lift up my request into your hands. May your will be done.

Amen,

_____

(Your signature)

After you write or print your final copy of your prayer request, place it in a spot where you will be subtly reminded of your request. This could be in a jar or basket, on a mirror or in your wallet or purse.

5. Pray.

In prayer, learn to follow the quiet voice within you that speaks in feelings rather than words. Follow what you feel inside, rather than what others may be telling you to do. Finish your request or prayer with a statement such as, "Thy will be done" or "This or something better." In doing so, you open your heart to possibilities that your conscious mind is unable to see. Let go and trust in God. You could also end your prayer request with a simple serenity prayer that will allow you to focus your energy on those things that you can influence or change.

> *God grant me the serenity to accept the things I cannot change;*
>
> *The courage to change the things I can;*
>
> *And the wisdom to know the difference.*

6. Let your intuition help guide you in determining if your specific prayer request is manifesting itself in one way or another.

God works in mysterious ways. Be open to all possibilities happening.

7. Always be in a state of gratitude should your request manifest itself.

Take a moment to thank God for the changes that are occurring in your life.

> He has achieved success who has lived well, laughed often and loved much; who has gained the respect of intelligent men and the love of little children; who has filled his niche and accomplished his task; who has left the world better than he found it, whether by an improved poppy, a perfect poem or a rescued soul; who has never lacked appreciation of earth's beauty or failed to express it; who has always looked for the best in others and given them the best he had; whose life was an inspiration; whose memory a benediction.
>
> **Bessie Stanley**

Let us put theory into practice by making an initial prayer request with the intent of aligning your life purpose with the goal of achieving spiritual success.

Taking into consideration steps No. 2-4, write your first draft of your prayer request below:

Dear God,

I would like help with _____

_____

_____

Please bless me by allowing those people, ideas, resources or opportunities to enter into my life so that I can:

_____

_____

_____

_____

_____

I ask that you give me this or something better as I lift up my request into your hands. May your will be done.

Amen,

FORMULATING MY TOP THREE SPIRITUAL GOALS

Take a moment to review the twelve points of consideration for goal setting, as well as the ideas and concepts presented in this chapter. Without being too judgmental or analytical, compose a list of eight to nine goals that could possibly be implemented to help you along your spiritual journey to total success:

	Possible goals for my spiritual development

Review each possible goal and ask yourself these three questions:
- Will this goal align me with my life purpose?

- Will this goal add value to people's lives?
- Will this goal allow me to reach my full potential?

If you are unable to answer yes to any of the three questions, consider setting aside this possibility as a goal right now. Once you have eliminated certain possibilities, take a moment to go back and rank each goal in order of priority from one to nine.

Rewrite your top three choices below.

Example: Starting tomorrow, I will read and reflect on one chapter each day, for the next forty days, from Rick Warren's book, *The Purpose Driven Life*.

Spiritual Goal No. 1: _____

_____

_____

Spiritual Goal No. 2: _____

_____

_____

Spiritual Goal No. 3: _____

_____

_____

Reflective journaling

Take a few minutes to think about the new concepts that you have learned and what you have learned about yourself. Jot down those thoughts and feelings below.

_____

_____

_____

_____

My Spiritual Life

CINDY'S SUCCESS TIPS FOR SPIRITUAL GROWTH

As you read each success tip, indicate whether it is:

A. a new idea for me to try

B. an idea that I need to research more

C. an idea upon which I need to improve

____ Take some quiet time each day in God's presence through meditation.

____ Learn about the positive attributes of various religions.

____ Get involved in a spiritual community such as your local church.

____ Seek out a study group to better understand God's Good Word.

____ Practice a daily devotion of reading and reflecting upon God's Word.

____ Become involved in missionary work either here or abroad.

____ Share your testimony as to how God has made a difference in your life.

____ Get into the habit of formulating prayer requests.

____ Watch programs dealing with religion and spirituality on television.

____ Listen to inspirational songs.

CINDY'S SUGGESTIONS

These resources may be purchased from your favourite bookstore or online.

Purpose-Driven Life by Rick Warren.
Grand Rapids, Michigan: Zondervan, 2002.
www.purposedrivenlife.com

The Road Less Traveled by M. Scott Peck, M.D.
New York: Simon & Schuster, 1978.
www.mscottpeck.com

Chicken Soup for the Soul: Living Your Dreams by Jack Canfield and Mark Victor Hansen.
Deerfield Beach, Fla.: Health Communications, 2003.
www.chickensoup.com

The 7 Habits of Highly Effective People by Stephen R. Covey.
New York: Simon & Schuster, 2004.
www.stephencovey.com

Day Three

My core relationships

> *What is the quality of my relationships like?*
> *How successful am I as a communicator?*
> *Who could help me achieve total success in my life?*

Let's take an initial look at where you are at in your understanding of relationships. In point form, fill in the left-hand side of the table below with as many concepts as come to mind. Once you have brainstormed for a few minutes, fill in the right-hand side with your queries. As you work through the material in this chapter, keep these questions in the back of your mind.

What do you know about relationships in general?	What do you <u>need</u> to know or find out about relationships?

The bottom line is that relationships are what really matter in this life. The key to successful relationships is being able to manifest unconditional love to those with whom you come in contact over the course of your life. Love does make the world go around. Unconditional, no-strings-attached love defines who we are as spiritual beings. We were made in God's image to be loving, caring, patient, compassionate beings. It is through your unconditional love for others that you gain true success in your life.

Receiving and giving unconditional love has many benefits to you, namely:

1. Being cared for and loved brings about great satisfaction for your human spirit.
2. Feeling loved creates a sense of high esteem or honor for the other person, which in turn creates increased feelings of self-worth.
3. Experiencing love has a positive affect on your emotional well-being, allowing you to experience a more positive attitude in your day-to-day activities.
4. Physiological changes occur, enabling you to better enjoy your physical health.
5. Enhancing the lives of those around you in creating relationships based on love increases your chances for having a long and prosperous life.

In order to enjoy the many benefits brought about by loving unconditionally and achieving total success in your life, you need to build and maintain strong relationships with those individuals closest to you.

IT ALL STARTS WITH EFFECTIVE COMMUNICATION

We are relational beings. Most of us seek out some form of social interaction and we take great pleasure in establishing positive, meaningful relationships with others. A key ingredient in all relationships is effective communication. Your verbal communication with someone involves skills in both listening and speaking. To be an effective communicator, you must have the abilities both to be a sympathetic listener and to actively engage another in conversation. Good communication doesn't just happen. You must spend the time and the effort in developing it. To create a sense of togetherness, both individuals need to learn to communicate their experiences, thoughts, feelings and desires in a friendly, uninterrupted, sympathetic context. Encouraging honesty and transparency in your conversations comforts others to open up and speak their minds. If you adopt a positive cooperative communication style, which fosters open genuine communication with others, you will experience growth in all your relationships.

What is a sympathetic listener?

It is hard to listen, even when you are interested, because people generally talk at about 125 words per minute and think at about 400 words per minute. Their thoughts move faster than the words of whatever they are listening to, so this is why a person's attention often wanders away from what another person is saying. We are not born good listeners. It is a learned skill. Hearing is a natural ability, but listening means focusing on what you are hearing and trying to make sense of it.

When you actively listen to someone, you are able to:

- learn from them
- express interest in them, giving them a sense of being valued
- gain insight into their needs, desires and motivations
- give them an opportunity to open up and gain your trust
- clarify misconceptions or fears they may have.

How do you work towards becoming a sympathetic listener? First of all, you need to listen with your eyes, which means that you will need to maintain eye contact with that person when he or she is speaking. Second, you need to listen with your body. Observe your body language. Are you engaged in other distracting activities? Are you square to the person? Are you sitting up and leaning forward slightly to show that you value what that person has to say? Use facial expressions and body language to express interest and comprehension. Third, listen without your mouth. In other words, avoid the temptation to interrupt while listening. Allow that individual time to express his or her thoughts, concerns, fears and insights. Avoid erecting barriers that get in the way of you hearing what is being said. Avoid over-reacting to highly charged or emotional words. Hear the person out. Avoid being hasty, biased, or prejudiced, or following a strict agenda and thinking that what you have to say is more important than what that person thinks or might want to say.

As you actively listen to someone, try to observe his or her body language for clues as to his or her feelings and true thoughts. Express your understanding with positive affirmations and by paraphrasing for clarification. Paraphrasing is restating a comment made by someone. Ask reflective questions (i.e. how, why, when, where, what, who) in an attempt to draw more specific information out of the conversation. Make every effort to concentrate on what is being said. Actively try to hear every word.

Your ability to connect with someone is directly related to how approachable you are. Active listening is something that we do out of caring and concern for others. Show genuine interest in what they have to say. Seek to clarify and understand. Try to leave each individual feeling better for having talked to you and for having shared his or her concerns and thoughts.

Reread this section on being a sympathetic listener and briefly identify five or six key points on how you could be a more sympathetic listener. Start each point with an action verb.

1. _____

2. _____

3. _____

4. _____

5. _____

6. _____

How should I actively engage someone in conversation?

At all times you should communicate with others using kind words spoken with an appropriate tone of voice. Sometimes our words are saying one thing, yet our tone of voice and posture indicates the contrary. You should be constantly affirming words of appreciation to others.

What are words of affirmation?

- *Words of encouragement.* Use words that inspire courage in others, just as a coach inspires his or her team. Coaches motivate their athletes towards taking positive action.

- *Words of praise.* Use words that make a positive assertion or statement that will build someone up. Positive reinforcement builds individuals up rather than tearing them down. Praise helps to raise one's self-esteem and self-worth.

- *Words of appreciation.* Use words that express sincere gratitude for someone who has done you a service or an act of kindness.

Incorporate the following expressions into your repertoire of affirmative statements:

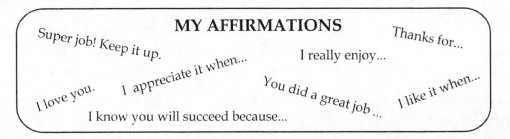

MY AFFIRMATIONS

Super job! Keep it up.
Thanks for...
I really enjoy...
I love you.
I appreciate it when...
You did a great job...
I like it when...
I know you will succeed because...

Do you find it easy or difficult to speak words of affirmation to others? Why?

_____

_____

What specific relationship could you enhance? _____

Make a list of the specific kinds of things you could say that would show appreciation, encouragement and praise:

1. _____
2. _____
3. _____
4. _____
5. _____
6. _____

Now, make a point of practicing and using these or similar expressions on a regular basis. Show recognition and appreciation and give praise. Catch someone doing something well and then pass on a few words of encouragement. Set a goal of giving a verbal affirmation to someone once a day over the next forty-eight days.

Spending quality time

Time has become a precious commodity in the twenty-first century. As a society, we spend less and less time with close family members. From the perspective of building meaningful relationships, we also tend to waste our time when we are in the company of others. With whatever time we do have, in order to foster creating healthy relationships, we need to maximize the use of our time. Emphasize spending quality time with your loved ones. Quality time means spending time doing something together that both of you enjoy doing, but more importantly it is the time spent creating a sense of togetherness. To create that sense of togetherness, both individuals need to learn to communicate their experiences, thoughts, feelings and desires in a friendly, uninterrupted, sympathetic context. Select quality activities that both are willing to do together. Both of you need to approach those activities with a positive attitude and an open mind. Focus not on what you are doing but on why you are doing it.

Make a list of individuals who represent your most important relationships.

1. _____   2. _____
3. _____   4. _____

5. _____ 6. _____

7. _____ 8. _____

9. _____ 10. _____

11. _____ 12. _____

Which core relationships should you develop?

Place a check mark beside the names of these individuals.

From your core list, who seems to be asking for quality time in your relationships?

1. _____ 2. _____

3. _____ 4. _____

What quality activities could you do to improve those relationships?

1. _____

2. _____

3. _____

4. _____

Now, be proactive. Take a look at your schedule or agenda and set aside some quality time this week to develop those core relationships. Get into the habit of scheduling a specific block of time for those important elements in your life.

> Good communication is as stimulating as black coffee, and just as hard to sleep after.
>
> **Anne Morrow Lindbergh**

SERVING OTHERS

A fundamental concept to realizing total success in your life is serving others in love. This goes against the prevailing general attitude of our North American society of focusing on "me" first. Your true love finds its expression in acts of service. Serving others must be done on a voluntary basis out of love, not out of fear or coercion, but out of choice. Being manipulated by another is not an act of love. It becomes an act of slavery. We all have certain God-given talents or spiritual gifts and skills that can be used to express love. Serving others can be as simple as performing an act of kindness to someone you see sitting on a sidewalk, working in your office, carrying groceries from the store or waiting in line.

How could you show acts of service to those closest to you? Jot down a few possibilities.

_____

_____

_____

_____

_____

Keep in mind that actions usually speak louder than words. Set a goal to perform an act of service every day to someone you care about over the next fifty days. Why fifty days? Remember, permanent physiological change in behaviour requires time to occur.

Through serving others with compassion, you become sensitive to others' struggles and needs. You begin to take an important step in becoming involved in someone else's life, not just your own. Show empathy for those less fortunate than you. Make a commitment to spend your time and energy adding value to their lives. Help them through their struggles and celebrate your successes together.

Serving others not only involves supporting individuals with their day-to-day struggles, but also helping develop their full potential. To be truly successful in this life, you need to help someone experience total success. Make people-development your top priority. Inspire others to follow their path to total success.

CONNECTING WITH MY FAMILY

How can I build a stronger relationship with my family members?

Keep the following four recommendations in mind as you work on realizing your specific action plan to building a stronger family unit:

1. Show appreciation for each other.

    Everyone deserves to be treated with respect and dignity. Feeling appreciated and valued brings out the best in each of us. In order to do so, you must create a supportive home environment. A supportive home is one that acknowledges individual differences, values others' strengths and yet understands others' weaknesses.

2. Strive to use words of affirmation and praise.

    We all feel better about ourselves when we receive positive feedback. Work together on fostering acceptance and unconditional love between all family members by using kind, affirming words. Build each other up, rather than tear one another down.

3. Commit to spending quality time together.

    If you do not make the effort to sit down and spend quality time with your family, the likelihood of finding it on the spur of the moment is slim to none. Our fast-paced North American society has imposed great pressures and challenges on how we spend our leisure time. Make spending quality time with your family a priority. Develop family rituals, traditions and special memories on a daily basis. It is not specifically what you do that counts, as long as you enjoy doing it together as a family unit.

4. Establish common family values.

    As a parent, you have a moral responsibility to instill fundamental family values as some of the core values described on Day One. Common values strengthen the family unit by providing direction. With older children, sit down and work towards identifying some common values that you can build on together as a family. Try to identify at least five things you are willing to fight for, or on which you are not willing to compromise.

My action plan

1. One of the first things you need to do for at least one month is cut back on watching trash TV and bad news. Do something radical for the next month and cancel your cable or satellite programming. What this will do is enable you to focus more time on developing rapport with family members. Replace TV time with building a stronger family. Start by talking about everyone's aspirations, values and goals. Make your conversations an opportunity to share and grow closer together.

2. Knowledge is power. Learning is a gift that you can develop together. Increase everyone's awareness of what is happening in this incredible world by learning about it. Listen to CDs and read books rather than watch mindless TV shows. If you must watch TV, focus on learning channel programs or support your local PBS station, which offers a multitude of value-based programs.

3. Our North American population is becoming more and more sedentary. Combat the urge to be a couch potato and commit to doing a family physical activity together. Try to make it something simple and inclusive, yet fun to do for all. You will develop greater bonds and enjoy the multitude of benefits that regular physical activity brings.

4. Make time to have fun together. Activities conducive to conversation such as puzzles, card games and board games are a great way to solidify family relationships.

5. Develop a sense of teamwork by working on certain chores together. It now becomes everyone's responsibility to pitch in, contribute and help each other in completing a specific task. With everyone working together, no one can complain about being treated unfairly or being picked on.

STRENGTHENING MY MARRIAGE

Develop a sense of unity in your marriage by setting aside some of your personal, self-serving desires for the good of the relationship. This means sacrificing some of your personal goals in order to develop ones common to the relationship. In marriage, two individuals commit themselves to each other. You share in each other's joys and sorrows and in each other's successes and failures.

On a regular basis and especially in the early stages of your marriage relationship, set aside a block of quality time together. Plan a weekend together away from the distractions of family, friends, work, television or the phone. Minimize those communication killers so that you may focus on each other. Give each other your undivided attention during your getaway to learn and grow together.

Marriage is a commitment and dedication to make the relationship grow and prosper. If you want to help each other, commit to building a marriage based on unconditional love, mutual respect and patience. Avoid trying to change your partner. In marriage, learn to accommodate each other and respect each other's major differences. As well, be patient with each other's patience. Developing patience takes time.

My action plan

1. What three specific areas in your marriage could you focus on during the next six weeks that will nurture more patience and help your relationship become more successful?

    a) _____

    b) _____

    c) _____

2. Make time in both of your schedules to go for a walk together at least twice a week over the next six weeks. During your quality time alone together, focus on positive things to talk about, rather than on problems or stressful topics. Celebrate your individual successes together.

3. Turn off your TV for the next month, select some books that will enhance your marriage relationship and spend the time reading and discussing.

BUILDING LASTING FRIENDSHIPS

Choose your close friends carefully. Associate with positive, success-driven people. Dissociate yourself from people who constantly drag you down with their negative, destructive attitude. Identify and remove yourself as much as possible from situations that drain your energy. Some of the toxic situations to avoid are: arguing, gossiping, backstabbing, mocking and accusing. On your total success journey, you want to attract individuals who will support, encourage and motivate you with their positive disposition.

Build relationships with those you trust. Choose to associate with individuals who demonstrate loyalty in the relationship, which means they are being faithful and true to you. There should be a level of commitment expressed by both parties to actively foster growth in the relationship. Seek to support each other through unconditional love. Cultivate integrity by being true to your word at all times. Walk the talk: Live and act truthfully. Avoid shading the truth by telling little white lies or by making statements that are true at one level but not necessarily true in the global context. Your relationships will prosper when you are open, honest and supportive of each other through the thick and thin of what life has to offer. Be resolved to spend quality time with your core friendships. Keep the communication channels open on a regular basis.

RESOLVING RELATIONAL PROBLEMS

Try to act quickly to resolve conflicts. Delay only strains relationships by increasing feelings of resentment, anger, frustration and pain. Your goal is to try and reconcile your differences first, then try to find a resolution to the problem. A good starting point is to use the power of forgiveness to set the tone of your meeting. Through forgiveness, you set aside those self-destructive emotions and you open yourself up to achieving greater success in reconciling your relationship. Not only do you come to terms with forgiving others, but also with forgiving yourself. Try to choose the right time and the right place to meet and discuss your differences. Ideally, you both want to be at your best and have adequate time to talk without distractions or interruptions.

Keep these following steps in mind:

1. Attack the problem, not the person. It all starts with establishing a supportive environment for finding solutions to deal with inappropriate behaviour, personal struggle or misunderstandings. Avoid withholding your love.

2. Approach your problem solving with a willingness to find a better solution between two people. Your goal should be to attempt to get all the facts before making any decisions. To do so, you will need to sympathize with each other's feelings and seek to understand each other's position. Be authentic in your desire to understand all sides of the story.

3. Discuss all the options you have come up with. Cooperate with each other to find common ground. There is always a way to find viable options, so leave your excuses at the door. Focus on where you want to go, not on where you were or where you are. You cannot change the past, but you can definitely learn from it.

4. Adopt a win-win attitude, where both parties feel that they have gained something positive in arriving at the best solution. You both must reach a point of consensus for this to happen.

5. Focus on using this particular experience as a learning opportunity, as opposed to dealing with a crisis. Use each of these confrontational experiences to learn more about yourself. Keep in mind that you are totally responsible for the experiences in your life. Choose to turn a problem around 180 degrees, and turn it into a learning opportunity.

ATTRACTING IDEAL PEOPLE

For most of us, going on a journey by ourselves is lonely and isolated. Having others be a part of your dream is much more fulfilling and rewarding. Your core group of relationships has a big influence on the level of success you will achieve. Ideally, you should try to surround yourself with wise, trusted and supportive individuals to whom you are accountable. Being accountable to someone for your actions and progress will enable you to become more successful in attracting more abundance and prosperity into your life.

Who will be on my success team?

The first step to attract the right people to help you succeed is making sure they are compatible with you. When taking others along on your total success journey, ask yourself two key questions about your choices:

- Do I like and admire them?
- Do I respect and trust them?

Pay attention to your gut feelings and intuition. Nothing puts a damper on pursuing your success journey more than associating with individuals you don't respect or trust. Don't settle for second best. By setting high standards, you set yourself up to attract more abundance, prosperity and ultimately, total success into your life. Ask yourself: Are these individuals capable of performing at the level I require in order to achieve my goals and dreams?

Here are words of wisdom that may help you select individuals for your success team:

- Associate with positive and successful people who will motivate and inspire you.
- Change your attitude about who you associate with. To achieve your goals, you may need to step

out of your network of peers and participate with new people in a higher level of networking status.

- Form a mental image of meeting the type of individual you would like to attract into your life.
- Learn to see and seize opportunities when they unfold. Adopt an attitude of making things happen.
- Look for individuals who value loyalty, who will be there for you when times are tough.
- Seek out leaders, individuals who know where they are going and are able to persuade others to go with them.
- Always look for individuals who are actively engaged in adding value to other people's lives.

Who could you include on your total success team?

Other than your immediate family members, write down the names of specific individuals who would be ideal candidates for helping you along your total success journey. In selecting prospects, try to select individuals who will support you in at least one of the six areas for total success.

1. _____   2. _____
3. _____   4. _____
5. _____   6. _____
7. _____   8. _____

Make a point of contacting your prospects within the next couple of weeks to discuss the possibility of having them support your endeavours.

You may also wish to formulate a specific prayer request asking for individuals who can help you along your success journey to manifest themselves.

My Core Relationships

Dear God,

I would like help with _____

_____

_____

Please bless me by allowing those people, ideas, resources or opportunities to enter into my life so that I can:

_____

_____

_____

_____

_____

_____

I ask that you give me this or something better as I lift up my request into your hands. May your will be done.

Amen,

_____

FORMULATING MY TOP THREE RELATIONSHIP GOALS

Take a moment to review the twelve points of consideration for goal setting, as well as the ideas and concepts presented in this chapter. Compose a list of eight to nine goals that could possibly be implemented to build your relationships and help you along your journey to total success:

	Possible goals for building my core relationships

Review each possible goal and ask yourself these three questions:

- Will this goal align me with my life purpose?
- Will this goal add value to people's lives?
- Will this goal allow me to reach my full potential?

My Core Relationships

If you are unable to answer yes to any of the three questions, consider setting aside this possibility as a goal right now. Once you have eliminated certain possibilities, take a moment to go back and rank each goal in order of priority from one to nine.

Rewrite your top three choices below.

Example: Today, I will turn off the television for a period of one month; instead, I will spend the time either talking with my family or doing a family activity together.

Relationship Goal No. 1: _____

_____

_____

Relationship Goal No. 2: _____

_____

_____

Relationship Goal No. 3: _____

_____

_____

Reflective journaling

Take a few minutes to think about the new concepts that you have learned and what you have learned about yourself. Jot down those thoughts and feelings below.

_____

_____

_____

_____

_____

CINDY'S SUCCESS TIPS FOR BUILDING RELATIONSHIPS

As you read each success tip, indicate whether it is:

A.   a new idea for me to try

B.   an idea I need to research more

C.   an idea upon which I need to improve.

_____   Take time to connect with your siblings on a regular basis.

_____   Mentor someone on his or her total success journey.

_____   Seek out an organization that develops public speaking skills.

_____   Make better use of your time through time management strategies.

_____   Become involved in a Mastermind group.

_____   Take a course with your spouse on building relationships.

_____   Attend a leadership development seminar.

_____   Set up a monthly dinner club with two or three other couples.

_____   Check out books or CDs that focus on building relationships.

_____   Get into the habit of scheduling all your core relationship activities on a monthly calendar.

CINDY'S SUGGESTIONS

These resources may be purchased from your favourite bookstore or online.

Five Love Languages: How to Express Heartfelt Commitment to Your Mate by Gary Chapman. Chicago: Northfield Publishing, 2004
www.fivelovelanguages.com

How to Get What You Want and Want What You Get by John Grey.
New York: Harper Collins, 1999
www.marsvenus.com

Secrets to Lasting Love: Uncovering the Keys to Lifelong Intimacy by Gary Smalley.
New York: Simon & Schuster, 2000.
www.garysmalley.com

Day Four

Expanding my mind

How do I most effectively expand my mind?
What does it take to improve my comprehension
and understanding of what I am learning?

Interestingly enough, we are all intrinsically motivated to learn and to achieve. We all have an inner craving to feel the satisfaction that comes with achievement. As learners, we also have a basic need to obtain a certain level of control over our lives. Knowledge provides that power. It allows each and every one of us to achieve the impossible. With the power of knowledge, we are able to seek more autonomy. Learning builds greater confidence in our abilities, leading to the desire for more independence. As we grow in knowledge, another basic human need, that of self-esteem, also grows. Through the successes of our achievements, taking control of our destiny, and the increased freedom and confidence in our decision-making, we develop a higher self-esteem. Not only do we think more highly of ourselves, but we also develop a deeper sense of self-worth in being able to give back to society what we have learned.

LEARNING HOW TO LEARN

Most of us have attended either public or private school in our younger, more formative years. Quickly, brainstorm below some of the positive experiences you gained through the educational system. What have you learned about expanding your mind?

_____
_____
_____
_____

Four basic principles used by smart learners

1. Learning is an active process that should involve as many senses as possible in making new connections to prior knowledge. You should constantly analyze and reflect on how you could adjust to your learning to reach your maximum potential. By establishing clear goals for your new learning, you provide motivation and an ability to retain more information. Your learning should be purpose-driven.

2. Learning should be a collaborative process where knowledge is shared between individuals. This not only enhances your life, but also allows others to collectively pool information and experiences that may eventually lead the entire group to achieve a higher understanding of an issue or specific concept.

3. As a learner, you are responsible for actively engaging yourself in the process and helping others make a positive contribution to their learning.

4. Smart learners seek to learn how to learn. By understanding how we can improve the quality and quantity of learning, we make it easier to head down the path to total success.

Conditions conducive to learning

Visualize your ideal learning environment. Either draw what you see in the space below or briefly indicate in point form what you see, hear, feel or sense.

To get the most out of time spent improving your mental capacity through either reading or listening, try to create these environmental conditions, which are conducive to learning:

- Set up a space or room devoted entirely to learning, either for reading books or listening to CDs.
- Select a quiet, secluded space with a table or desk and comfortable chair.
- Make sure that you have good lighting. Proper lighting is crucial to being able to reach high reading speeds.
- Incorporate steady, soft background noise or music when reading. The mind is not as easily distracted by sudden noises when it has adjusted to a certain amount of "white" background noise.

Ten tips for improving your mental capacity

1. Have a positive, "will try hard" attitude all the time. Engage yourself in the learning process. Commit to learning something new every day. Be proactive and develop some positive daily learning habits. Set aside some time each morning to stimulate and challenge your mental capacity by reading for fifteen to twenty minutes. Challenging your mind on a daily basis has been shown to slow down or protect against the onset of age-related mental decline.

2. Show a willingness to learn. Be teachable and keep an open mind to learning about the incredible world around you. Learning forces you to step out of your "comfort zone" and change the way you think about yourself, others and this world.

3. Ask, listen and learn. Use the acronym A.S.K. – Always Seeking Knowledge – to guide you. The bible says: Ask and you shall receive, seek and you shall find, knock and it shall be opened unto you. Let your curiosity take hold of you and move you to another level of understanding about yourself and your purpose on Earth.

4. Be creative in how you squeeze learning time into your daily routine. Can you combine your exercise time with reading or listening to a personal development tape?

5. Be organized and tidy. Keeping your desk area and learning resources tidy fosters both increased productivity and greater motivation to stay engaged in the learning process.

6. Avoid the time waster of blaming yourself or others for mistakes you make. Mistakes result in learning. Focus on learning from your failures.

7. Think of ways to apply what you have learned. Where could you use this knowledge? With whom could you share it? Also, continuously engage your mind in solving problems or overcoming obstacles in order to achieve greater success.

8. Make a point of moving your body every thirty minutes, should you be inactive while reading print material or listening to CDs. If you have been sitting for any length of time, get up and

stretch, walk around and grab something to drink. This will prevent your body from becoming both mentally and emotionally disengaged from the learning process.

9. Creatively engage your imagination. Take the printed or spoken word and visualize what the text represents. Build upon your images, adding details as more and more information is made available.

10. At the end of each day, reflect on what you have learned and all those little successes you have experienced. Record these thoughts and reflections in the journal section of your guide.

> Change does not necessarily assure progress, but progress requires change. Education is essential to change, for education creates both new wants and the ability to satisfy them.
>
> **Henry Steele Commager**

READING THE RIGHT WAY

How do you read a magazine as opposed to instructions for assembling your new computer desk? Are the two purposes for reading the same?

Before you begin to read a document, establish your purpose for reading the material. Are you reading for pleasure and just skimming over most of the material or are you trying to get an in-depth knowledge of something? How you read should depend upon your purpose at that moment.

Sub-vocal linear reading

Most of us use what is called sub-vocal linear reading.

This has two dominant characteristics, namely:

a) You accompany your reading by using a "hidden voice" that pronounces the printed words silently or as a barely audible murmur. The words are sounded out in your head.

b) You read from left to right, line-by-line, horizontally across the page.

Sub-vocal linear reading has one major drawback – a maximum reading speed of about 900 words per minute. A typical sub-vocal linear reader reads at about 300 words per minute. In contrast, should you develop a visual-vertical technique, you can reach speeds of over 5,000 words per minute while maintaining reading comprehension. Before we discuss the main concepts of visual-vertical reading technique, let us focus on how to improve our sub-vocal linear reading fluency.

One of the biggest areas of improvement to our reading fluency involves minimizing or avoiding these four common practices:

- moving your lips or vocalizing the words as you read. Your reading becomes inefficient because this practice slows you down to a conversational speed of about 125 words per minute.
- reading each word one after the other. In doing so, you lose both reading fluency and comprehension of the entire passage.
- backtracking or going back over what you have just read. Usually this is a symptom of inattention or inefficient reading practices.
- using the same reading rate for all material, rather than adjusting your rate according to the nature and difficulty of the text.

The following tips will help improve both your reading fluency and comprehension:

1. Select an environment conducive to learning – one that is quiet, has few distractions and is comfortable.
2. Carefully break in your book so that it is easier to turn the pages without losing your place. To do so, place the spine of your book, as well as the front and back covers, on a flat surface. The pages will fan upwards. Carefully flatten a few pages at a time by the spine as they flop down on either side of the spine towards the desk.
3. Become an active page-turner as you read. Sit up straight to facilitate both efficient page turning and enhanced concentration. Have your page-turning hand in a position to turn each page quickly so as not to break your reading rhythm.
4. Ensure that you are able to see each page in its entirety. This means you need to adjust your body position, ensure adequate lighting and wear properly prescribed glasses, if need be.
5. In the beginning, use an underlining hand motion as you read. This allows you to coordinate your eye movement with your hand at a predetermined pace, which prevents your eyes from stopping on single words or backtracking over what you have just read. Try to decrease the frequency by which these regressive movements occur. Also avoid the temptation to go back and reread every word that you may have missed on the first pass. Eventually, with practice you may be able to develop the necessary eye control to eliminate your need for hand scanning.
6. Enlarge your vocabulary as much as possible by paying attention to new words and using your dictionary or thesaurus.

Visual-vertical reading

It is not the intent of this book to teach you how to use visual-vertical reading. However, it may be useful to gain a little insight into this reading technique, which you may wish to explore in further detail at a later date. The two underlying principles of this accelerated reading technique are that you must learn to:

a) accept and trust your eyes as you read, and avoid using your "hidden voice"

b) read vertically down the page as opposed to across the page.

"Accelerated" readers are able to take in more words at a glance than the average reader. They have also learned to quickly shift their focus from one group of words to another without extraneous eye movement. To become an "accelerated" reader, you will need to develop a conscious and deliberate control over your eye movement across the page, as well as expand your vision consciousness area or eye span, so that you may take in more than just a few words at a time. With intensive and extensive practice, it is possible to change old habits and dramatically improve reading speed.

READING COMPREHENSION AND REMEMBERING LONGER

Have you ever finished reading something, only to discover that you didn't understand what you just read?

Our understanding or comprehension of what we are learning can be greatly improved by focusing on a few key comprehension strategies, as follows:

1. Get an overview of what you are going to read before you start reading. Browse through the material, looking at all headings, bold or italic type, bulleted sections, lists, pictures and tables. Skim over anything that stands out from the ordinary text. In doing so, you end up with an idea of where the material is going to take you and you will be in a better position to make connections.

2. Make connections: As you read or listen, try to use your existing knowledge about the subject area to help you make sense of what you are learning. Attempt to make connections between what you already know and the new information.

    a) What you have read or heard about may be related. What are other related concepts that you have already assimilated?

    b) Connections stem from your own personal experiences. How do these ideas apply to your life? Can you find an emotional "hook" to the new information?

    c) Your global perspective of the world may also trigger connections. How does this new information fit in with your understanding of the world?

3. Create visual images: Imagine a whole picture of the new concept. Visualize how it would look, feel, sound or behave. As mentioned previously, engaging as many sensory experiences as possible in your understanding of new ideas or concepts helps commit them to long-term memory.

4. Read with specific questions in mind: Keep your mind actively engaged by asking yourself questions before, during and after reading or hearing the information. Your inquisitive mind should be formulating higher-level thinking questions that incorporate who, why, when, where, what and how. These questions should stimulate an inner desire to discover more in-depth answers. The right questions will enable you to associate the new material being presented with your own personal experiences and knowledge base, thus making retention easier and forgetting virtually impossible.

5. Determine what is important: Try to determine what the main idea and key supporting details or concepts are within each passage that you listen to or read. Are these details essential to the development of the main idea being presented?

6. Apply what you have just learned to your own personal experiences. In using this new information four or five times in the context of your present understanding, you create lasting memories by integrating the old with the new.

SOURCES OF INFORMATION

A wealth of knowledge is found in all sorts of venues and individuals. Some of these are shown below. What sources do you already use on a regular basis? Check those that apply and add any not listed.

	Public library		Specialty television channels
	Book stores		Public radio stations
	Internet book distributors		Personal coaches
	Commercial websites		Mentors
	Personal internet blogs		Workshops and seminars
	Commercial book clubs		Continuing education programs
	Local book clubs		Conferences
	Study groups		Trade shows
	Video rental stores		Post-secondary institutions
	Public television		Successful entrepreneurs

Expanding My Mind

Choose three specific sources of information that you currently do not use on a regular basis and that you would be interested in pursuing.

1. _____

2. _____

3. _____

Who could you possibly talk to in order to better connect with your three new information sources? When will you contact them? Write your commitment down on your monthly calendar or agenda.

1. _____

2. _____

3. _____

"When you stop learning, you stop living."

"Your continued pursuit of knowledge gives you life."

FORMULATING MY TOP THREE LEARNING GOALS

Take a moment to review the twelve points of consideration for goal setting, as well as the ideas and concepts presented in this chapter. Compose a list of eight to nine goals that could possibly be implemented to help you expand your mind while on your journey to total success:

	Possible goals for expanding my mind

Review each possible goal and ask yourself these three questions:

- Will this goal align me with my life purpose?
- Will this goal add value to people's lives?
- Will this goal allow me to reach my full potential?

If you are unable to answer yes to any of the three questions, consider setting aside this possibility as a goal right now. Once you have eliminated certain possibilities, take a moment to go back and rank each goal in order of priority from one to nine.

Rewrite your top three choices below.

Example: This week I plan to either purchase or borrow a book on improving my memory and I will practice some of the memory strategies every day for the next month.

Learning Goal No. 1: _____

_____

_____

Learning Goal No. 2: _____

_____

_____

Learning Goal No. 3: _____

_____

_____

Reflective journaling

Take a few minutes to think about the new concepts that you have learned and what you have learned about yourself. Jot down those thoughts and feelings below.

_____

_____

_____

_____

_____

CINDY'S SUCCESS TIPS FOR EXPANDING YOUR MIND

As you read each success tip, indicate whether it is:

A. a new idea for me to try

B. an idea I need to research more

C. an idea upon which I need to improve.

_____ Take some quiet time each day to read material that is stimulating, challenging or informative and related to your chosen career.

_____ Learn how to increase your reading speed through a course or book.

_____ Discover the art of studying. Pick up a book or enroll in a course.

_____ Seek out a book club or study group that would enrich one of your passions.

_____ Read and reflect upon a daily devotion of God's Word.

_____ Become involved in a public speaking organization, so that you may more effectively share your knowledge.

_____ Read one book each month that would help you on your total success journey.

_____ Listen to at least one personal development CD each month.

_____ Enroll in a personal development seminar at least once a year.

_____ Watch selective documentaries shown on PBS or a learning-oriented station.

CINDY'S SUGGESTIONS

These resources may be purchased from your favourite bookstore or online.

Improving Your Memory: How to Remember What You're Starting to Forget by Janet Fogler.
Baltimore: John Hopkins University Press, 2005
www.amazon.com

Remember Everything You Read:
The Evelyn Wood Seven Day Speed Reading and Learning Program by Dr. Stanley D. Frank.
New York: Avon Books, 1992
www.evelynwood.com

Improving Your Study Skills by Shelley O'Hara.
Hoboken, N.J.: Wiley Publishing, 2005.
www.amazon.com

Day Five My physical well-being

What does it take to benefit from a healthy lifestyle?

How does my physical well-being impact my relationships?

How can I schedule regular physical activity into my daily routine?

Your physical well-being has a significant impact on how effective you are in growing to your maximum potential and in adding value to people's lives. In order to reach your full potential, you need to understand how your physical activities, eating habits and health practices influence each other. The balanced interplay that must exist between your physical fitness, nutrition and health determines the extent of your physical well-being.

Being physically fit does not mean that you have reached a point of physical well-being. You may be fit, yet not healthy. For example, you could be suffering from an injury or illness as a result of overdoing a specific activity. In this chapter we will explore some of the key positive influences you can control in order to reach a point of physical well-being. Keep in mind that one of your objectives in working through this guide is to learn how to develop each of the six areas leading to a level of balance in your life that ensures that you will achieve total success.

What prior knowledge do you already have about how you could improve your physical well-being?

Based on what you already know from your life, print material that you have come across, information in the media, and specific situations or events in the world around you, list some specific steps that you could or should take to improve each of the following areas:

Physical activity and fitness	Eating habits and nutrition	Health, stress, and healing

What are the benefits of a healthy lifestyle?

Research has shown that adopting a healthy lifestyle prevents, treats or lowers your risk of developing cardiovascular disease, diabetes, certain cancers and osteoporosis. Physiological changes occur in the body that help to lower both high blood pressure and cholesterol levels. Regular physical activity coupled with good nutrition builds and maintains healthy organs, muscles, bones and joints, as well as a healthy body weight. Your healthy lifestyle promotes a sense of well-being by relieving excessive stress. You are able to perform simple day-to-day tasks with ease, having enough energy left over to enjoy the company of others, your favourite pastime, or making a significant difference in this world.

> A healthy body is a guest chamber for the soul: a sick body is a prison.
>
> **Francis Bacon**

The foundation of life, long health and well-being involves establishing positive health habits. It is never too late to make significant changes to your life, no matter what your age. Start today in making changes necessary to enjoy life to the fullest.

Focus your attention on the following:

1. Stay up-to-date with immunization shots.
2. Get periodic medical examinations or health screenings from a health professional.
3. Make regular physical activity a part of your life.
4. Have a balanced, nutritious diet.
5. Pursue healthy pleasures every day. Enjoy life to the fullest. Laugh.
6. Stay mentally active. Learn something new every day.
7. Completely avoid pleasure-inducing or illegal drugs.
8. Stop using tobacco products. It is never too late to stop smoking or chewing.
9. Limit your alcohol consumption.
10. Manage your stress through exercise and relaxation techniques.
11. Use your prescription drugs wisely.
12. Take care of your teeth with regular oral hygiene and dental checkups.
13. Take safety precautions at home and work to reduce accidents and injuries.
14. Help make this a healthier world. Celebrate your wisdom with others.

BASIC FITNESS PRINCIPLES

A good fitness plan has three essential components: aerobic endurance, muscular strength and flexibility. Working towards building all three areas enables you to have balanced fitness and move closer to realizing your optimal level of physical well-being.

The Essential Three

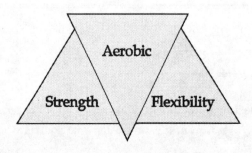

Aerobic endurance is the body's ability to deliver oxygen and nutrients to major muscle groups engaged in prolonged activity and to eliminate waste by-products of exercise as they are being produced. Your aerobic fitness allows you to do more throughout the day with less fatigue.

Strength is the ability of a muscle group to exert a large amount of force over a short period of time. Strengthening your muscles enables you to lift or move objects with greater ease and to perform these tasks longer before fatigue sets in.

Flexibility refers to the body's ability to freely move body parts over a full range of joint motion. Being able to stretch your muscles prevents injury and promotes greater balance.

How does the body change with physical activity?

Physical activity places increased demands on several systems in the body, such as the musculoskeletal, cardiovascular and immune systems. Through physical activity, the body is required to function at a higher level of performance. It is during the recovery and rest phase after exercise that the body adapts to the increased stress that was placed on it by making minute physiological changes. These physiological changes increase the efficiency of the various systems that were initially involved in the physical activity.

Where do I start?

Your primary focus for developing your fitness level should be on improving your cardio-vascular system through aerobic endurance activities. This provides the foundation from which both the strength and flexibility components may be better developed.

Aerobic activity for the beginner

Simple steps for building your aerobic endurance:

Step One: Ensure that the activity that you choose to build your cardiovascular system is an aerobic activity. Is this activity or sport:

a) steady and non-stop?

b) putting your heart rate into your target heart-rate zone?

   See the Target Heart Rate Zone page at the end of this chapter for specific details.

c) lasting at least twelve minutes in your target heart-rate zone?

d) using large muscle groups?

AEROBIC ACTIVITIES

walking, cycling, paddling, snowshoeing, rowing, running, stair climbing, jogging, kick box cardio, hiking, cross-country skiing, aerobics, swimming

Step Two: Choose a physical activity or sport that you enjoy. The top three activities I could pursue on a regular basis are:

1. _____ 2. _____ 3. _____

Step Three: Take the initiative. Pull out your agenda or calendar now. Set aside a block of thirty minutes tomorrow and get out and be active. Start slowly and at an easy pace. Your body requires time to adapt. In the beginning, you may even try combining light activity, such as walking, with moderate activity, such as jogging.

Step Four: Exercise in your target heart-rate range for at least twelve minutes. Monitoring your heart rate ensures that the intensity of the activity is appropriate to maintain for an extended period of time.

Should you choose to exercise with others in the beginning, ensure that they have similar fitness levels. Fit friends may end up pushing you too hard. Developing new, positive habits requires time. Try to stay committed to a regular exercise routine. If you miss a day, pick up from where you left off and don't worry about it.

You should begin to see positive changes occurring after the first two weeks in:

- establishing the new positive habit of exercising regularly
- overcoming the initial mild discomfort of moving your body in a way in which it may not be accustomed. These minor physiological adaptations by the body usually pass within a short period of time.

You may see noticeable physiological changes to your body within the first six weeks of following your exercise routine. Such changes may occur in:

a) how easy a previous exercise intensity level has become as your body is able to do the same workload at a lower heart and respiratory rate

b) how quickly your body is able to decrease its heart rate, respiration rate and blood pressure after exercising

c) how much more energy you have for your day-to-day activities.

By the time you reach Day Fifty of your total success program, you will have established another positive routine that will enable you to further grow to your full potential.

A typical aerobic exercise routine

Warm-up	Stretching	Activity	Cool down	Stretching
5-10 minutes	5-10 minutes	12-60 minutes	5-10 minutes	5-10 minutes

<u>Warm-up</u>: Start your routine with five to ten minutes of light aerobic activity. Your warm-up allows your body to slowly increase its core temperature, which increases blood flow to the muscles and loosens up the joints. This reduces the risk of injury. Focus on your technique and performance, allowing your mind to shift its thoughts from any worries or stresses to the benefits and pleasure of your activity.

<u>Stretching</u>: Spend between five and ten minutes slowly stretching the major muscle groups that will be used during your activity. Hold each stretch without bouncing for ten to twenty seconds. Relax and breathe deeply as you stretch. Never stretch to a point of discomfort or pain.

<u>Activity</u>: Ease into your activity. Try to maintain your heart rate in your target zone. Monitor your heart rate by taking your pulse every five to ten minutes in the beginning, less frequently as you learn to "read" your body.

<u>Cool down</u>: Make a point of taking five to ten minutes of light activity after your main aerobic activity to flush your body of certain toxins that have been produced during exercise and to allow your body to ease your heart rate, blood pressure and breathing rate down.

<u>Stretching</u>: To maintain or increase your flexibility, take five to ten minutes after cooling down to slowly stretch all the major muscle groups of your body. After your exercise routine, your muscles are tired and fatigued, which is an ideal time to stretch with less risk of injury.

Within twenty minutes of finishing your routine, hydrate your body with two to three glasses of water or a fluid replacement drink. Keep in mind that the physiological changes to your body occur during your recovery period after you exercise. It is imperative that you replace the fluid and nutrients your body has lost during exercise, while in a restful or relaxed state.

Strength training

Besides aerobic conditioning and flexibility development, strength training is another essential ingredient to include as part of your total fitness program.

Strength training increases your muscular strength and endurance, which is necessary for day-to-day independent living. Throughout the day, you require muscular strength and endurance to lift and move objects, or even to get up in the morning. One major benefit of strength training is that you will see positive changes to your physical appearance as a result of body composition changes. Your body will appear firmer and fitter. As your musculoskeletal system grows stronger, your posture will improve. As a result of all these changes, your self-confidence will soar.

Ten tips to setting up your strength training routine:

1. Organize your strength or weight training routines in the same way as your aerobic routines with a warm-up, initial stretch, workout, cool down and final stretch.
2. Plan a rest day in between each workout. Muscle repair and growth takes longer between workouts when strength training.
3. Learn proper safety, technique and etiquette when lifting weights. Consult a qualified or certified trainer.
4. Be patient. You may experience mild muscle soreness in the early stages as the body adapts to your routine.
5. Seek immediate professional advice should you experience pain or prolonged muscle soreness.
6. Give yourself adequate time to learn the ropes. With time, what was intimidating and uncomfortable will become familiar and routine.
7. Consider joining a gym or taking a course to learn the basics.
8. Monitor your progress with a log that helps you keep track of the details of your exercise routine.
9. Consult your family when scheduling your workouts. Maintain a healthy balance in your relationships.
10. Devise a way to regularly reward yourself as you make progress and reach specific target goals.

Use these two guidelines to help you put together your total fitness program:

Aerobic exercise

<u>Initially</u>: three to four times per week for twenty-five to sixty minutes at a moderate intensity, which is sixty to seventy percent of your target heart rate.

<u>Eventually</u>: three to five times per week for fifty to sixty minutes, with at least two workouts being higher intensity or interval training (seventy to eighty-five percent of your target heart rate).

Strength training

Two or three times per week for thirty to sixty minutes. Make sure you don't exercise the same muscle groups two days in a row. Unlike aerobic exercise, muscles being taxed through strength training require longer to recover.

Using the sample one-week fitness program as a template, plan your next week's fitness activities below. The total exercise time commitment includes warming up, cooling down and adequate stretching.

Sample fitness program	
Sunday	Off
Monday	Strength workout at the gym: 45 minutes
Tuesday	Trail jog/run: 40 minutes
Wednesday	Mountain bike: 60 minutes
Thursday	Strength workout at the gym: 40 minutes
Friday	Kayak: 45 minutes
Saturday	Long, slow distance jog/run: 80 minutes
My fitness program for next week	
Sunday	
Monday	
Tuesday	
Wednesday	
Thursday	
Friday	
Saturday	

Many of us have a hard time squeezing our exercise routine into our daily routine or weekly schedule. Here are some practical suggestions that may help you:

1. Take the stairs or walk more often.

2. Use your lunch hour to get fit.

3. Get up before the family does to work out.

4. Buy a push mower or use your rake and shovel more often.

5. Volunteer in your community as a coach.

6. Squeeze in a workout right after work before heading home to your family.

7. Exercise while watching TV or reading on a treadmill or exercise bike.

8. Perform a five-to-ten minute stretching/strengthening routine while taking a break at work.

9. Cycle or run to work or when you need to do errands.

10. Play with your kids at the park or share your exercise time with your family.

> Happiness is a state of activity.
>
> **Aristotle**

Being consistent in following your fitness routine is the most important part of becoming fitter. In order to get the most benefit from your routine, use these guidelines to help you stay motivated:

1. KISS—Keep It Simple to Succeed: Keep the logistics of doing the sport or activity as easy as possible, such as: clothing requirements, travel arrangements, weather dependency and equipment preparation.

2. Pace yourself. A comfortable and safe progression encourages continuation of your routine.

3. Feeling too tired to get into your routine? Push past your initial mental resistance and just get out the door. Often it is the lack of exercise that makes you feel tired. Exercise will energize your body.

4. Focus on the long-term benefits to you, your family and others as a result of the positive changes fitness brings about for your total success.

5. Engage all of your senses and enjoy what you are doing, seeing, hearing, smelling or feeling. Take pleasure in what you are experiencing.

6. Enlist the help of other positive role models or mentors to keep you motivated and focused.

7. Be accountable. Use an exercise diary or an accountability partner to keep you on track.

8. Change your routine if you sense that you are becoming bored. Sometimes a little variety is all you need to spice things up.

9. Faced with bad weather, either dress appropriately for the activity or set up your program so that you have a choice between indoor and outdoor activities.

10. Now, pick a simple fitness-related goal that you think you can reach this week. Think of progressing in baby steps. Start today and keep track of what you do. When you reach your goal, reward yourself. Then, set a new goal.

"A healthy lifestyle can be as contagious as the common cold.

However, don't wait to catch it from others.

Be a carrier."

NUTRITION

What is a balanced, healthy diet?

A healthy eating practice is one that provides your body with the essential nutrients it requires to build, maintain and repair cells, as well as provide you with adequate energy to pursue your life to the fullest. It is balanced in that the majority of the foods are selected from each of the following four major food groups:

1. Grain products

Choose whole grain and enriched products more often as they are high in starch and fibre. Some examples of good choices are brown rice, whole-wheat pasta, multigrain bread and cereals with three grams or more fibre per serving. Try to include five to twelve servings in your meals each day. A typical serving size is the amount of food that will fit in a small cup or in the palm of your hand.

2. Fruits and vegetables

Choose dark green and orange coloured vegetables and orange coloured fruits more often, since they are higher in key nutrients such as vitamin A and folacin. Eat fresh fruits and vegetables most of the time. Avoid deep-frying. Try to consume five to ten servings per day.

3. Milk products

Choose lower-fat milk products more often, such as skim or one percent milk, cheeses containing less than twenty percent milk fat or yogurt containing less than two percent milk fat. Milk products provide high quality protein and calcium. Drink or eat two to four servings per day.

4. Meat and alternatives

Choose fish, poultry and lean cuts of meat. Eat a variety of lentils, dried peas and beans as well. Soybean products are also a great source of protein. Instead of frying food, try baking, broiling, roasting or microwaving. Eat two to three servings per day.

Ideally, you should eat a variety of foods from each of the four major food groups in moderation four to five times per day. Eating smaller quantities of food more frequently provides the body with a steady supply of nutrients, which then can provide a constant supply of energy to meet all the demands of your day.

Both Cindy and I try to follow Canada's Food Guide to Healthy Eating from Health and Welfare Canada, which can be obtained online at www.hc-sc.gc.ca/index_e.html.

Ten tips to healthy eating practices

1. Stay hydrated. Drink lots of hydrating fluids, preferably six to ten cups of fluids such as water, juice or milk, throughout the day.
2. Limit your consumption of alcohol to no more than two glasses per day.
3. Limit your caffeine consumption to the equivalent of about four cups of coffee per day.
4. Limit your intake of salt to cut back on the negative effects of excessive sodium, which can raise your blood pressure. Most processed foods contain an adequate amount of sodium necessary for life. Leave the saltshaker on the shelf.
5. Choose low-fat and more natural snacks, such as dried fruit, crackers, vegetable sticks or bagels.
6. Should you follow a vegetarian diet, ensure that you are eating a variety of legumes, soybean products, grains, seeds and vegetables in order to give you all the essential amino acids necessary for protein synthesis.
7. Limit your intake of processed foods and drinks containing sugar.
8. Eat breakfast. Provide your body with the necessary nutrients and energy to get you going.
9. Avoid diet pills, fad diets and weight loss programs that offer a short-term solution. Ask yourself: Would I be able to follow this diet for the rest of my life?
10. Limit your intake of fast food, which is high in fat or sodium.

My Physical Well-being

ACHIEVING OPTIMAL HEALTH

Having a healthy body means you are able to:

- efficiently manage life's little stresses
- be free of disease
- have energy and enthusiasm to reach your full potential
- achieve an inner sense of peace and harmony.

We all experience the effects of both positive and negative stressors throughout the day. You cannot avoid stress in your life but you are able to choose how you react to it.

In dealing with situations or circumstances that create a lot of negative emotions or stress in your life consider the following:

- Relieve tension through physical activity or by getting a massage.
- Use relaxation techniques to bring about a sense of inner peace.

Consider learning one or several of these techniques to help alleviate stress:

1. Specific, focused deep-breathing exercises

Learn how to practice this technique first. Proper breathing techniques enable the heart rate, respiratory rate and blood pressure to lower. Your focus will be on oxygenating the brain and body while calming the mind.

2. Meditation

This is a combination of both relaxing breathing techniques and engaging the mind in calming reflection or contemplation. The focus of meditation is on clearing the mind of extraneous thoughts and may be used to achieve a greater spiritual connection to God.

3. Yoga

This is a practice that combines postures, relaxation, breathing and meditation techniques to achieve a harmonious development between the body and mind. Yoga postures promote the elimination of toxins in the blood. Muscles become toned and joints are kept flexible. Yoga is not a religion. People from all walks of life have practiced it for thousands of years in India.

Many books, tapes and CDs have been created in order to teach you how to use various relaxation techniques. Consider checking them out at your local bookstore or online on the internet.

Dealing with illness

Your immune system is responsible for suppressing and eliminating infection caused either by viruses or by bacteria. A healthy immune system is able to handle these invading agents, but when it becomes compromised or weakened, illness follows.

Keep these suggestions in mind when you are dealing with illness in your life:

1. Get an adequate amount of rest each day, which includes about eight hours of sleep each night. Try to go to bed early as opposed to later in the night in order to optimize your recovery. Your body needs down-time to re-energize, build up its immune system and fight infection or disease.

2. Drinking water on a regular basis throughout the day is essential to flushing toxins out of your body. Coupled with this is maintaining good nutrition and eating five or six low-calorie meals spaced out over the day. Eating frequently places less strain on the body and provides a continuous stream of nutrients.

3. Consult your doctor, pharmacist or homeopath about supplements or homeopathic remedies that may boost the immune system.

4. Be aware of environmental triggers that could aggravate allergies or upper respiratory diseases such as asthma. Regulate the relative humidity in your home or office with dehumidifiers or humidifiers at forty to fifty percent. Improve air quality in your home with frequent vacuuming, dusting and bedding changes. Consider getting your heating system cleaned annually.

5. Engage your mind in the healing process. Maintain a positive attitude that the steps you are taking to deal with your illness will restore your body to a healthy state. Align your intention to strengthen your immune system with God's desire for you. Let go and let God.

Avoiding injuries

Most injuries are classed as either acute or overuse. An acute injury occurs suddenly when stress is applied abruptly. Overuse injuries occur gradually over time. To reduce the risk of injury at work or at play, take the following proactive approaches:

- Listen to your body. Heed any warning signs of overuse such as pain, frequent discomfort and unusual stiffness or tenderness. Reduce your activity level, allowing the body time to repair any damage.

- Avoid radically changing your exercise routines, especially the type and intensity of activity. Allow your body time to gradually adjust to the demands of the activity. Be aware of the negative effects of improper footwear or running surfaces on your lower body.

- Consider using a cross-training approach for your exercise program. Engage in a variety of activities or sports that exercise all of the major muscle groups. Balance weight-bearing activities such as running and aerobics with non-weight-bearing activities such as swimming, cycling and cross-country skiing.

FORMULATING MY TOP THREE PHYSICAL WELL-BEING GOALS

Take a moment to review the twelve points of consideration for goal setting, as well as the ideas and concepts presented in this chapter. Compose a list of eight to nine goals that could possibly be implemented to help achieve physical well-being on your journey to total success:

	Possible goals for my physical well-being

Review each possible goal and ask yourself these three questions:

- Will this goal align me with my life purpose?
- Will this goal add value to people's lives?
- Will this goal allow me to reach my full potential?

If you are unable to answer yes to any of the three questions, consider setting aside this possibility as a goal right now. Once you have eliminated certain possibilities, take a moment to go back and rank each goal in order of priority from one to nine.

Rewrite your top three choices below.

Example: Starting today, I plan to establish a daily routine of being physically active by walking to and from work, as well as to and from the store.

Well-being Goal No. 1: _____

_____

_____

Well-being Goal No. 2: _____

_____

_____

Well-being Goal No. 3: _____

_____

_____

Reflective journaling

Take a few minutes to think about the new concepts that you have learned and what you have learned about yourself. Jot down those thoughts and feelings below.

_____

_____

_____

TARGET HEART RATE ZONE

As a beginner, use the following guidelines when you are exercising:

Age	Target Heart Rates				
	50%	60%	70%	80%	85%
20	100	120	140	160	170
25	98	117	137	156	166
30	95	114	133	152	162
35	93	111	130	148	158
40	90	108	126	144	153
45	88	105	123	140	149
50	85	102	119	136	145
55	83	99	116	132	141
60	80	96	112	128	136
Please consult your physician when starting an exercise program should you be over 60.					

Monitoring your heart rate or pulse

To take your pulse, using your first two fingers (never your thumb), lightly press your fingertips into the right-hand groove of your neck just under your jawbone. Take your pulse for a count of ten seconds. Multiply your count by six to give you an estimated heart rate per minute. While taking your heart rate, try to keep your breathing, muscular movements and pace regular or constant in order to get a true indication of your exercise intensity.

At some point in time in the future, you may wish to invest in a heart rate monitor to electronically calculate your pulse and display your beats per minute on the screen of the special watch worn. Heart rate monitors are an easy and accurate way to monitor your heart rate while exercising. Monitors come with a variety of features and range in price from sixty to several hundred dollars.

CINDY'S SUCCESS TIPS FOR PHYSICAL WELL-BEING

As you read each success tip, indicate whether it is:

A.   a new idea for me to try

B.   an idea I need to research more

C.   an idea upon which I need to improve.

____   Keep track of your physical activity in a training diary.

____   Explore the benefits of yoga, pilates or martial arts.

____   Learn more about homeopathic medicine.

____   Start practicing relaxation techniques on a daily basis.

____   Set a goal of participating in a community fitness event.

____   Join a health and fitness club.

____   Hire a personal trainer.

____   Invest in some simple home exercise equipment.

____   Fine-tune your aerobic exercise with a heart-rate monitor.

____   Set up your healthy eating program in consultation with a nutritionist.

CINDY'S SUGGESTIONS

These resources may be purchased from your favourite bookstore or online.

Body Break: Keep Fit and Have Fun by Hal Johnson and Joanne McLeod.
Mississauga, Ontario: Body Break Inc., 1999
www.bodybreak.com

One on One with Tony Little: by Tony Little.
New York: Berkeley Publishing Group, 2003
www.tonylittle.com

Body for Life: 12 Weeks to Mental and Physical Strength by Bill Phillips.
New York: HarperCollins Publishers, 1999
www.bodyforlife.com

Getting in the Gap: Making conscious contact with God through meditation by Dr. Wayne W. Dyer.
Carlsbad, California: Hay House Inc., 2003
www.hayhouse.com

Day Six

My emotional development

How do my beliefs affect my attitude?

How do I develop a great attitude?

How could I better control my negative thoughts and feelings?

MY BELIEFS INFLUENCE MY ATTITUDES

Each of your beliefs is based on an assumption that something is true. But beliefs you've created can be changed to intentions that better support your journey towards total success. Everything in life is a choice. No matter what happens to you in life, you choose how you perceive what is unfolding. Your choices establish attitudes that influence daily rituals, which in turn produce the results that you see in your life. If you are unhappy with the results, look first at whether your current beliefs are aligned with your life purpose and the goals you have established for yourself.

To get a better understanding of how you can change your non-supportive, limiting beliefs, let us look at what shapes your beliefs.

Your current beliefs are based on:

1. your upbringing within your family and what you have heard and seen while growing up. What are a few current beliefs you hold that were instilled at an early age by your parents? (Example: Get an education. Get a job. Work hard.)

_____

_____

_____

2. circumstances that have unfolded in your life—specific incidents that have helped shape what you believe in. What current beliefs have resulted from specific events in your life?

_____

_____

_____

3. the limitations presently imposed on your life as a result of being born into a certain socio-economic class or culture. How has your culture and social status impacted your beliefs?

_____

_____

_____

4. what others say and do. Your family, friends, colleagues and society in general shape your beliefs through diverse opinions expressed, different values communicated and certain attitudes asserted. How have society's values shaped your current beliefs about the world around you?

_____

_____

_____

We make decisions each and every day based on our beliefs. The emotions or feelings associated with these thoughts and decisions create either supportive or non-supportive attitudes. Supportive attitudes are positive in nature and based on the premise that the universe is an unlimited source of abundance. On the other hand, a non-supportive attitude is grounded in fear and the notion that scarcity in the universe is the norm.

Your current attitudes shape your actions and lead you to make choices between desirable habits and bad or destructive habits. Habits are certain behaviours you keep repeating to the point where they become automatic. For example, I have a habit of exercising every day. Success-oriented habits create positive rewards. Negative habits breed negative consequences, which may not show up until much later in your life, such as the effects of smoking or excessive eating.

Developing new habits takes time. Small, positive adjustments to your behaviour may occur in as little as two to three weeks. Ingrained habits may require months to change. Be patient with yourself. Focus on systematically improving one behaviour at a time. You may be tempted to slip back into your old ways. Stay the course despite any minor setbacks. Developing positive, supportive habits will dramatically change your lifestyle and move you closer to achieving total success.

One of the first steps to changing non-supportive behaviour or a habit is realizing it is holding you back from achieving more abundance and prosperity in your life. Once you have identified the culprit, you can focus on understanding how your thoughts have created this non-supportive situation and work towards adopting supportive thoughts and feelings. In choosing to change your thoughts and feelings, you change your attitude, which in turn changes the behaviours that ultimately affect the results you seek.

What are the signs of having a great attitude?

People who have great, positive attitudes believe in themselves and others. They are able to focus on opportunities, not obstacles, and are persistent in finding solutions to challenges. They have an innate desire to give of themselves and their resources to make this place a better world.

How can I improve my attitude?

1. Take full responsibility for your thoughts, choices and life. Stop making excuses or justifying your actions. Excuses are just negative beliefs. Successful people avoid making excuses. Are your excuses an indication of hidden fears or are they real? Has anyone else successfully overcome the situation you're using as an excuse?

2. Associate with positive people. In doing so, you develop the supportive habits that attract abundance into your life. Try to build an excellent support network.

3. Live in the present. Focus on what you can change in the moment, not on what has already passed or could happen in the future. Live your life to the fullest in joy and gratitude one day at a time. Life should be fun.

4. Engage in stress releasing activities every day, whether physical or mental. Relieving stress has a positive impact on both your mental and physical health.

5. Take positive steps towards changing your attitude. Actions speak louder than words. Identify and focus on those actions that bring about a positive attitude in you.

6. When negative circumstances manifest themselves, look at this new challenge as an opportunity to learn and grow. Make the best of the situation and keep moving forward along your path to total success. Never give up.

7. Learn from your failures. We all experience the temporary setback of failure. How we react to our mistakes and misfortunes determines whether or not we will become successful. Don't take your

failures personally and let them get you down. Seek to either correct your mistakes or learn from them. As well, look at your failure in terms of the big picture and your life purpose. Try not to take life so seriously. Adopt a positive, humorous perspective. Rather than look at the failure, focus on the lessons you learn that could make you more successful.

8. Take baby steps. Establish short-term goals you can accomplish within a week or month. As well, get into the habit of celebrating your accomplishments on a daily basis.

MY ACTION PLAN

Setting boundaries

One of the first steps to attracting more abundance and prosperity into your life is to clearly determine what boundaries you need to establish both at home and at work.

Establishing boundaries allows you to spend time only on projects or behaviours that make a real positive difference in your life or the lives you touch. Establishing boundaries focuses your attention on the essential matters that support your total success journey. Learn to say NO to elements that distract you from achieving your goals. Four of the top distracters to avoid in order to stay the course are:

- Other people's intentions for you and their expectations of you. Focus on what is aligned with your goals and life purpose. Don't be drawn into doing something that is not aligned with what you have established as your personal goals and life purpose.

- Interruptions from the telephone. A word of advice: unplug your phone or turn off your cell phone at meal times and when you are spending quality time with someone. Meal times are for developing your relationship with your spouse and family. Give your undivided attention to those you love and care for.

- Excessive TV watching. Rather than becoming a couch potato, become an active learner. Pick up a book, listen to a tape or share your knowledge with someone. The greater your knowledge, the easier it is for you to realize your dreams and attract abundance and prosperity into your life.

- Becoming a workaholic. We have all heard the expression: "All work and no play makes Jack a dull boy." Strive to establish balance between all six major developmental areas in your life. It is important to schedule specific quality time to develop your relationships with family and close friends. It is also very important that you set aside time for your own personal growth and development, whether that be spiritually, physically, mentally or emotionally.

What specific boundaries could you establish that would help create better balance in your life right now?

1. _____

2. _____

3. _____

4. _____

Developing positive habits and rituals

One positive habit you can develop right now is that of questioning and challenging your beliefs, as to whether they support your higher purpose and your goals. To develop a positive habit, you must first have an open mind and embrace change before you take an honest look at yourself. In the space below, list the key habits that are holding you back from realizing your dreams and attracting abundance and prosperity into your life.

1. _____

2. _____

3. _____

4. _____

5. _____

6. _____

7. _____

8. _____

9. _____

From your list, select the three most important habits that are having a negative impact on your life. Indicate some of the negative consequences of these habits. What are the specific benefits or payoffs of eliminating or changing these negative behaviours?

Negative habits	Consequences	Benefits of changing

Our habits establish the daily rituals that allow us to manifest our attitudes. Our rituals provide the necessary balance between our energy expenditure and recovery. As we have seen with physical fitness, the body expends energy during activity, but growth and positive adaptation occurs during rest and recovery. Our mind is no different. How can you change your top three negative habits to make them more supportive, positive and beneficial?

1. _____

2. _____

3. _____

Visualization exercise

Close your eyes and take a moment to visualize the benefits and rewards you will reap. Create the images and feelings associated with these new positive habits.

Feel what you want to attract. Now feel thankful and grateful for these positive changes. Focus on aligning your intentions with God's intentions for you.

Twelve declarations to change your mindset

A declaration is a verbal statement of intention to either be or do something. To be effective, a declaration needs to be a positive affirmation stated aloud in a formal manner with physical actions.

The more senses that we engage in the learning process, the easier it will be to create permanent change. As silly as this may sound, stand in front of a mirror to jest and smile as you make your declarations. Have some fun changing your mindset.

Practice the twelve declarations on the following page twice a day, preferably once in the morning and once at night, for the next two months. You will be amazed at how effective this technique is in changing your beliefs and attitudes.

Learn from positive individuals

What better way to get an idea of which attitudes to adopt to become more successful than to observe and learn from individuals who have already developed several supportive attitudes and habits. In talking to successful individuals, ask questions, listen attentively and take notes so as not to forget key points.

Who could you interview to gain some insight into success-oriented habits?

1. _____

2. _____

3. _____

Now, make a commitment to contact one of these individuals within the next week, so you can schedule some chat time with them. Take a moment right now to place his or her name in your agenda or on your calendar. Remember:

> Talk is cheap; actions produce results.

My Emotional Development

MY TWELVE SUCCESS ATTITUDES

1. I am richly blessed every day since my life purpose is aligned with God's higher purpose for me.

2. I deserve to have more abundance and prosperity in my life because I add value to other's lives.

3. I am truly grateful for all the people, experiences and opportunities that have come into my life.

4. My legacy is my unconditional love for others.

5. I spend quality time and use effective communication in nurturing my core relationships.

6. I attract the ideal people into my life who support my efforts.

7. I am open to constantly learning and improving my mental capacity.

8. My healthy lifestyle gives me optimal physical well-being.

9. My total success attitude guides my actions to produce the results that allow me to reach my full potential.

10. I choose to create the beliefs and attitudes that support my dreams.

11. My multiple streams of income allow me to be financially free.

12. I constantly seek lucrative opportunities to leverage both my time and money.

IDENTIFY AND ADDRESS YOUR FEARS

A common acronym for FEAR is *f*alse *e*vidence *a*ppearing *r*eal. Most fears with which you are faced every day are not real but imaginary, having been created from your thoughts and feelings. Your fears create doubt and worry, which in turn destroys your self-confidence. We all face fears. How we address our fears determines how successful we become. Unsuccessful individuals let fear stop them dead in their tracks. The negative emotions associated with fear drain energy from your body and prevent you from reaching your maximum potential. Turn this negative state around, learn to identify and confront your fears head on. Let us do so right now.

Step One: Identify your fears

What do you really fear the most? What do you fear right now and in the future? Make a list of the fears that are holding you back from being successful, keeping in mind each of the six areas for total success. Try to identify fears in each area.

1. _____
2. _____
3. _____
4. _____
5. _____
6. _____
7. _____
8. _____
9. _____
10. _____
11. _____
12. _____

My Emotional Development

Step Two: Question your fears

Visualize what would actually happen if your fears came to pass. Now ask yourself two questions: "Could I survive?" and "Could I make a comeback?" Take a moment to address each fear you have listed in this manner.

In all likelihood, the chance you will rise from your failures or setbacks is very high. This reflective thinking process leads us to the next defining question: "What are the benefits to me in overcoming each fear?" Think how addressing each fear might help you achieve greater personal development and realize your dreams. List the specific benefits that will occur from addressing and overcoming each fear.

1. _____
2. _____
3. _____
4. _____
5. _____
6. _____
7. _____
8. _____
9. _____
10. _____
11. _____
12. _____

Step Three: Accept your fears

Having identified those fears getting in the way of your total success, you must now confront them. Addressing your fears means you must move out of your comfort zone and act in spite of fear and discomfort. Life is all about choices. Choose to accept and set aside your deepest fears. Decide from this point forward to act and move forward towards realizing your dreams. Everything you want in life is on the other side of your fears.

Step Four: Control your fears

What could you do to overcome each fear? Your first task is to focus on elements you can control from within you, as opposed to elements in your external environment. You may not be able to control your current living and working conditions or the actions of others, but you can control your attitudes.

What are some elements you can control that feed your fears?

1. _____
2. _____
3. _____
4. _____
5. _____
6. _____

Decide now to work on these specific elements and let go of external elements you are unable to control.

Step Five: Take action — strategies to deal with fear

We create protective barriers in our mind to maintain what we have grown accustomed to, or the status quo; we avoid change. When we change our subconscious mind, it requires both time and effort before adaptation occurs. This change is in the form of reprogramming our beliefs and adopting beliefs and attitudes that support our dreams and goals in life. By making a conscious decision to change our thought process, then following up with specific actions that involve as many senses as possible, we can confront and overcome fears.

Should you have to deal with the negative emotions evoked by addressing one of your fears, try using one of the following strategies:

<u>Positive self-talk</u>: By repeating key words and expressions that focus on positive outcomes, you can break through the fear barrier that your mind has placed in front of you. Imagine that you are talking directly to your inner subconsciousness.

Try using some of the examples below that both Cindy and I have used with success. To change your negative thoughts, focus on repeating supportive ones.

> I can do it! I believe in myself.
>
> Stay the course. Focus on my dream.
>
> Thank you for sharing. Now let's move on.
>
> Positive thoughts bring me the benefits and outcomes I desire.

<u>Fear declaration</u>: By using a series of formal, verbal statements, you can start to reprogram your mind to use positive, supportive thought patterns. Try memorizing and using the following statements to actively engage your mind and body in the change process:

> We are all faced with fear. I choose to confront my fears head on and act in spite of my fears.
>
> We all endure failure. When I fail, I will learn from my experience and use it to move me closer to achieving my total success.

A word about your ego

Your ego can get the better part of you in preventing you from attracting abundance and prosperity. Let go of your need to always be right, to always win, to be superior, to have more power, or to have more possessions and material wealth. When you allow your ego to control your actions, you lose sight of God's plan for you. Your ego can effectively *Edge God Out* of your relationship and your connection to this higher power and authority.

Stress relief

Worry and doubt bring about negative effects on your body, both mental and physical. Most chronic diseases are psychosomatic, brought about by the negative, non-supportive thoughts in our minds that create negative stress, which leads to disease.

When stress enters our lives, we can manage its effects better when we have adopted a positive, proactive approach to dealing with it.

Three proactive strategies to deal with stress:

- Find pleasure in humour. Laugh a lot. Don't take life too seriously.
- Practice meditation in order to calm and refocus the mind.
- Enjoy the stress-releasing benefits of physical activity.

"Take a moment to think about those things that bring joy into your life. Make a point of connecting with as many of them as possible, as often as possible, each and every day."

MY EMOTIONAL DEVELOPMENT

FORMULATING MY TOP THREE EMOTIONAL DEVELOPMENT GOALS

Take a moment to review the twelve points of consideration for goal setting, as well as the ideas and concepts presented in this chapter. Compose a list of eight to nine goals that could possibly be implemented to help develop a great attitude while on your journey to total success:

	Possible goals for my emotional development

Review each possible goal and ask yourself these three questions:

- Will this goal align me with my life purpose?
- Will this goal add value to people's lives?
- Will this goal allow me to reach my full potential?

If you are unable to answer yes to any of the three questions, consider setting aside this possibility as a goal right now. Once you have eliminated certain possibilities, take a moment to go back and rank each goal in order of priority from one to nine.

Rewrite your top three choices below.

Example: For the next six weeks, I will practice my success declarations every morning and evening.

Great Attitude Goal No. 1: _____

_____

_____

Great Attitude Goal No. 2: _____

_____

_____

Great Attitude Goal No. 3: _____

_____

_____

Reflective journaling

Take a few minutes to think about the new concepts that you have learned and what you have learned about yourself. Jot down those thoughts and feelings below.

_____

_____

_____

_____

_____

_____

My Emotional Development

CINDY'S SUCCESS TIPS FOR EMOTIONAL DEVELOPMENT

As you read each success tip, indicate whether it is:

A. a new idea for me to try

B. an idea I need to research more

C. an idea upon which I need to improve.

_____ Pick up a book on humour and spend a few minutes every day reading it.

_____ Attend a personal development seminar focusing on attitudinal change.

_____ Hire a life coach to work with you one-on-one.

_____ Practice visualization and meditation on a daily basis.

_____ Learn how to deal with your procrastination.

_____ Practice positive affirmations and declarations each morning and evening.

_____ Seek professional counselling to better cope with feelings of depression.

_____ Listen to motivational tapes, CDs or DVDs.

_____ Take in a stress-reduction workshop.

_____ Master your time pressures.

CINDY'S SUGGESTIONS

These resources may be purchased from your favourite bookstore or online.

The Success Principles:
How to Get from Where You Are to Where You Want to Be by Jack Canfield and Janet Switzer.
New York: HarperCollins, 2005
www.thesuccessprinciples.com

The Power of Intention: Learning to Co-create Your World Your Way by Dr. Wayne Dyer.
Carlsbad, CA: Hay House. 2004
www.drwaynedyer.com

Your Road Map For Success: You Can Get There from Here by John C. Maxwell
Nashville, Tennessee: Thomas Nelson, 2002
www.yourroadmapforsuccess.com

The Attractor Factor:
5 Easy Steps for Creating Wealth (or Anything Else) from the Inside Out by Joe Vitale.
Hoboken, N.J.: John Wiley & Sons, 2005
www.attractorfactor.com

Day Seven

My finances & career

What are the basic rules of investing?

How do I create multiple streams of income?

How could I better leverage my time and money?

Money management and finances are two of the most misunderstood, frustrating and poorly taught concepts in our society. Most of what we learn about money, and the attitudes we develop around money, come from either our parents and immediate family or from the school of hard knocks. The lessons we learn from the school of hard knocks are the day-to-day experiences we encounter regarding money in the real world. What does the concept of money mean to you? How do you view money? What attitudes do you associate with money? Take a moment to complete each of the following statements:

Money is _____

Wealth is _____

Getting rich is _____

Financial freedom is_____

Investments are _____

To be rich, I _____

As you work through this chapter, you have an opportunity to challenge and reshape some of your current beliefs about money. The choice is yours. As with any learning opportunity, please keep an open mind to the strategies and concepts being presented. In having an open mind, you move beyond your initial fears and into the realm of possibilities and opportunities that will attract more abundance and prosperity into your life.

WHAT IS FINANCIAL FREEDOM?

Financial freedom involves reaching a point when your passive income exceeds your expenses to support the lifestyle to which you would like to become accustomed. Passive income is money earned without actively working, such as through real estate rental income, stock dividends or royalties. You need not trade your time to make money. It is being generated 24/7. Reaching a point of financial freedom could be as simple as living within the means of your current lifestyle, or as extravagant as being able to travel extensively without worrying about how much you spend. In either case, your attitudes about your finances and career determine whether you will be able to reach a point of financial freedom and enjoy the lifestyle you desire.

TWO KEY ATTITUDES TO BECOMING FINANCIALLY FREE

1. Contentment

Being content with yourself means that you are:

- happy regardless of whether you have a lot or a little
- proud in making a worthwhile contribution to society
- self-confident about who you are
- free of the pressures of acquiring material things in order to prove yourself.

We live in a debt-ridden, materialistic culture that has been heavily influenced through marketing endeavours that stir up feelings of discontentment and promote self-gratification. This attitude of "buy now, pay later" has gripped most of our financial institutions. Many of us have been caught up in the "more is better" mindset. We need to change our attitude about what we do with our money, as well as what truly makes us content. The first step is to be content with what God is doing in your life. Ask yourself: "What would it really take for me to be able to enjoy my life to the fullest and be content?"

2. Patience

Most bad debt, debt that does not produce any income, stems from a lack of patience. Being able to wait and put off making a purchase until there is enough cash on hand is a difficult but necessary choice to become financially free. Despite the ease of being able to borrow money and finance any of our purchases, we must realize that it comes with a cost down the road – our financial freedom. Once again, to be truly successful in life, you need to achieve balance and harmony in each of the six areas discussed in this guide, which includes your financial success.

Reaching a point of financial freedom in your life requires patience in saving and investing your money,

My Finances & Career

patience in learning about various types of income streams and patience in persevering with working towards your specific financial goals.

Adopting these two key attitudes sets you up to make positive choices that support your efforts to achieve total success.

Your success is all about choices in life. Which of the following could you reduce (R) or possibly eliminate (E) in order to facilitate reaching your financial freedom sooner? Place the appropriate letter in the space before each area that you could change.

____ junk food

____ lunch or dinner in restaurants

____ fine wines and spirit

____ expensive diet programs

____ specialty coffees

____ perfume, makeup or hair care products

____ the latest fashions

____ cable or satellite TV services

____ club memberships

____ recreational vehicles and equipment

____ expensive vehicles

____ using your vehicle to travel everywhere

____ cost of your home

____ elegant furnishings and decorations

____ sports season tickets

____ phone services

____ the latest computer equipment

____ electronic equipment: music, games

____ home entertainment centres

____ expensive schooling

____ cost of a cottage or second home

____ music CDs and DVD film collections

Having identified some areas where you can cut back, let us now take a look at several simple strategies that will help you manage your money better.

MY MONEY MANAGEMENT STRATEGIES

Your financial success can be boiled down to the answer you give to one question: "How well do I manage my money?" Begin today to take better control of your financial affairs. Create the positive habit of effectively managing your money, no matter how much you start with. Read each of the five numbered statements aloud, as a positive declaration. Put some feeling and emotion behind it.

1. "I will involve my whole family in the learning process."

Engage your whole family in learning about how to effectively manage money. Don't keep your financial affairs or investments a secret. If you truly believe that your life purpose is to add value to other people's lives, then include all your family members in learning about finances. Ongoing communication about your financial matters is an absolute must if you would like to establish trust, security, individual accountability and a sense of financial peace within your household. When discussing financial matters with your spouse or family members, focus on active listening with both your body and your heart.

Within the next couple of weeks, arrange a financial date with your spouse, accountability partner or mentor. Block out enough time to ensure you can discuss matters openly without distractions or time pressures. Your goal should be to review the specific details of your financial records, reports, policies and budget to gain an in-depth understanding of where you are. Before you are able to change how you manage your money, you need to know what areas could be improved.

2. "I will reduce my debt load and expenses while increasing my savings."

Could you decrease your expenditures and be content with getting by with a little less? List three to five areas you could cut back on right away that would allow you to reallocate the money not spent to increase your savings over time.

1. _____
2. _____
3. _____
4. _____
5. _____

Reducing your debt load may be a long-term goal, but once you eliminate the heavy burden of bad debt, you can begin accumulating wealth. As a general rule, attempt to save ten percent of your net earnings every month. You may need to build up to this level of contribution slowly, as you also work towards reducing your debt. Make saving a priority in your life and the lives of your family members. Once your savings begin to accumulate, move them out of low interest-bearing accounts and invest in high interest-bearing financial instruments.

3. "I will gain peace of mind with my emergency fund."

There is nothing like being worry free of knowing how you will pay for the next crisis down the road. Your goal is to build up enough reserve funds over the course of the next year to cover three to six months of your normal expenses. Start by opening a savings account or money market account that doesn't penalize you for deposits and withdrawals. Initially, call this your emergency account, which is used to buffer your expenses when unexpected events happen. Eventually, you will also be able to set aside savings for long-term projects such as vacations, post-secondary education or projects around the home.

4. "I will create balance in my money management plan."

Both Cindy and I have used this particular money management plan with great success, because it allows us to build up our savings and rewards us every month for our efforts. Start by setting up separate accounts for each of the following categories and allocate funds in accordance with the recommended amounts:

10% of your net income for investing in your financial freedom

Imagine that you have just acquired three "financial freedom goslings." These are no ordinary goslings, but ones that eventually produce golden eggs. Your responsibility is to feed your little golden geese every month, building up your capital in various investments. Eventually you will be able to use the golden eggs, which form your interest earned from investments, to support your desired lifestyle. At no point in time should you kill any golden goose by spending the capital that you have already invested. You may reallocate capital to finance a project that is going to create wealth, but avoid the temptation to pay off any expenses.

10% for your education

Your financial literacy is fundamental to becoming a wise investor. Many people believe that certain types of investments are very risky. It is not the investment vehicle that is too risky; it is the unknowing investor. In order to reduce your risk, you need to develop good financial and business knowledge and skills. Your goal is to learn how to convert earned income into several passive income streams. This knowledge may be gained from a variety of sources, such as home self-study courses, workshops, seminars, conferences, books, magazines, CDs, websites and investment clubs.

10% for giving

Giving not only brings joy to others; it also brings you a sense of gratification in knowing that you are adding value to other people's lives. Get into the habit of supporting your community and helping those in need by giving a portion of your earnings away each month to a worthy cause. Give freely from your heart, not out of a sense of obligation.

10% for your emergency fund and future projects

As outlined above, setting aside money to cover any unforeseen expenses gives you peace of mind. Once you are able to set aside the equivalent of three to six months of expenses, you will be in a position to save for long-term projects.

10% for play

Life should be enjoyed now and through retirement. A secret to managing money well is establishing balance between hard work and rewarding yourself. Your play account should be spent each month on ways that rejuvenate your body and spirit such as a weekend getaway for two, a meal in a classy restaurant or a day at a health spa.

50% for necessities

The majority of your monthly financial obligations or expenses falls into this category. Make a concerted effort to reduce your expenses in the early goings by cutting back on certain luxuries or desires. The first key factor to getting ahead is coming to an agreement with your spouse about how you will manage your financial affairs, including your long-term financial goals. The second key factor is in slowly reducing both your debt load and expenses while increasing savings for purchasing various investments. Be patient with the process. It takes time to fatten your golden geese, but it is well worth it down the road.

5. "I will monitor my money management."

My cash flow analysis

An important aspect of controlling your money and being successful in the world of finances is keeping tabs on your cash flow on a regular basis. Your cash flow analysis is a written plan of how you spend your money. It is a simple cost-breakdown of your expenses, as seen in most budgets, and involves tracking your income and expenses on a monthly basis. Your cash flow analysis should take into account several important factors, such as:

- your budget priorities as a family, based on your passions and dreams
- the impact of your specific family values on your cash flow
- specific short-term budgeting plans, as well as long-term projections over a six-month to one-year period

Both Cindy and I have found that the easiest way to keep track of our cash flow is to use a simple electronic spreadsheet, available for free at www.YourSelfHelpTeam.com. Click on the Resource link. The most significant advantage in using an electronic spreadsheet is that you are able to see the effects of purchasing decisions being made today on your cash flow five or six months out.

Tracking my net worth

Besides monitoring your cash flow, it is important to periodically assess your net worth. The measure of true wealth is not in how many material possessions you have acquired. True wealth is a function of the relationship between your assets, or money flowing into your "piggy bank," versus liabilities, where money is being emptied from your "piggy bank." To calculate your net worth, you need to total up the assets you possess and subtract your liabilities. Assets typically show up in categories such as investments, bank accounts, pension plans, chattels or equity in your personal residence. On the other hand, liabilities include such categories as credit card debt, long-term loans, home mortgage, taxes owing or unpaid bills. We suggest that you calculate your net worth right now and then monitor your net worth every three to four months. Most financial institutions and financial planners will be able to help you keep track of your net worth, either by charting your assets and liabilities on paper or by entering this information into an electronic spreadsheet. Keep in mind that what you focus your attention on will increase. If you monitor your cash flow and net worth you will see positive change occurring within a very short period of time.

HOW DO I BECOME FINANCIALLY FREE?

Once you have your financial affairs in order and you are committed to saving a portion of your income each and every month for investment purposes, the next step is to look at how you can reach a point of being financially free. Financial freedom is attained when you do not need to rely on others or trade your time in order to pay for your desired lifestyle. That is where developing a personal plan made up of specific strategies and a simple automatic formula comes in. Investing is not a specific investment product or procedure. Investing is a system that focuses on how well your strategies are working, not on the specific results of your stock portfolio or marketing efforts.

There are two basic types of income:

Active income: typically income derived from working at a job where you trade your time to earn money. You must be actively involved in the process in order to generate this type of income.

Passive income: typically income that comes from sources such as real estate, stocks, marketing or businesses where your presence and direct involvement are not necessary for you to create results. This type of income is being created while you sleep or are on vacation.

Words of advice on getting ahead

1. Get into the habit of regularly converting your active income into passive income by acquiring assets.

2. Develop enough knowledge in each type of investment vehicle that you use so that you are prepared for whatever happens, whether markets go up or down.

3. Investigate before you invest. Do your due diligence with every opportunity before committing. Don't just blindly follow the masses.

4. Learn how to evaluate the risk to your capital versus the return on your investment. Reduce that risk by becoming financially literate.

5. Dedicate the time and energy to become financially free. Focus on education first, then the experience.

6. Everything has a price. Your time is more precious than money. Invest your time in learning about business and finance, and the opportunities to make money will appear.

7. Should you find a good opportunity, ask yourself: "How can I afford this?" Focus on attracting money. Be creative. Think outside the box.

8. Look for opportunities where you can ethically leverage using other people's money, resources and time. Do not take advantage of others for your personal gain.

9. If you do not own a business, start a part-time business. Being a business owner gives you the best chance of attaining wealth. Keep your day job while building up your new business.

10. Become an entrepreneur. Use your creative mind to build your assets, not your physical labour. Learn how to promote yourself, your ideas and your products or services with passion.

11. Set up an ongoing, active investment plan. Learn how to keep your money moving in and out of better and better investments, rather than just parking your money and forgetting about it.

12. Include investments in oil, gas and renewable energy sources, as well as precious metals, especially gold, in your investment portfolio.

13. Never take a job for just the money. Take a job only if you will benefit in the long term from the knowledge and skills you obtain.

14. Information and technology are doubling at a phenomenal rate. Be open to challenging your present notions and ideas, since what may have been right for you yesterday may not be so tomorrow.

15. On Day One you identified possible candidates for your total success team. Business is a team sport. Take your team with you into the world of business.

My golden geese

We have all heard the advice to not put all our eggs in one basket in case some unforeseen calamity should destroy all those eggs. Ideally, you want to be able to remove your eggs from a variety of baskets. This is the concept of diversification. Your focus should be on diversifying your investments in three wealth creation sectors, namely the stock market, real estate, and business & marketing. From within these sectors your "golden geese" will be able to produce your "golden eggs", which in essence are your multiple streams of income.

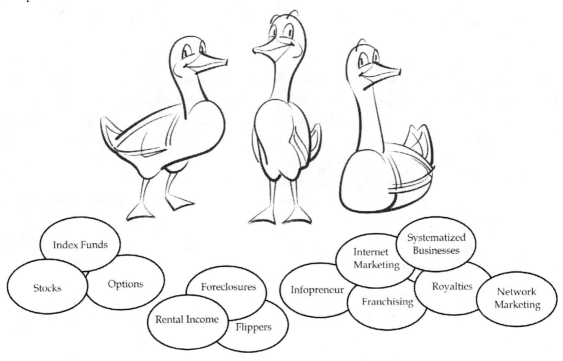

Your first step to financial freedom is learning about the various investment vehicles available to you, such as stocks, index funds, real estate rental property, royalties or systematized businesses, which run even when you are not present.

The next step is to invest your savings in the wealth creation sector in which you have the greatest knowledge base. As your learning progresses and you gain confidence, begin diversifying your investments into the other two wealth creation sectors. Get into the positive habit of investing slowly as your knowledge increases, as well as consistently fattening your golden geese.

Why become an entrepreneur?

Back in the Middle Ages, a dramatic change in the structure of society slowly evolved. The general population saw the emergence of the middle class. People began to go into business for themselves, becoming self-employed. They sold their goods and services, increased their wealth in doing so and thereby rose in social status. During the Industrial Revolution, we observed the rise of major corporations, which employed thousands who worked at a job for someone else, their employer. Very few of these workers were able to become wealthy or make significant positive changes to their lifestyle by working for someone else. Just as in the Middle Ages, your greatest chance of attaining great wealth or reaching financial freedom lies with being an entrepreneur.

An entrepreneur is a visionary or dreamer able to create a business that addresses a specific need in the marketplace. Successful entrepreneurs are able to either systematize their business so that they do not need to be physically present to run the operations or they collaborate with or hire individuals who in working as a team are able to do the majority of the work. A successful entrepreneur's focus is converting active income from the business to passive income with as little effort as possible. If you have created a business that depends on your presence to run, you are working at a job. If you are working at a job, your income is linear; for every hour that you invest in the business, you can expect a certain amount of money coming in. Strive to move beyond this limiting business model. Consider how you could create recurring or ongoing income streams, where money flows into the business whether you are present or not.

By becoming an entrepreneur and owning your own business, whether part-time or full-time, you benefit from the following major advantages over just working at a job:

- Becoming an entrepreneur provides you with yet another great learning opportunity. In striving to become a great business person, you have a greater chance of adding value to the lives of those around you by sharing both your knowledge and resources.

- We live in the Information Age today. It is possible to take new ideas and information into the marketplace and become wealthy or financially free. No longer does it require hard physical work and lots of money to create wealth. Making money has now become more of a mental than physical process.

- Business owners are given more tax incentives than are employees. Those who work the hardest physically are paid the least. As well, they usually end up paying the most taxes, because they are not able to benefit from the tax advantages of owning their own business.

- Owning a business enables you to use pre-tax dollars for investment purposes. You are able to buy more assets with your gross income than with your net income. Employees are placed in a situation where taxes are withheld from their total income, thereby reducing the amount of money they are able to invest up front.

- Being an entrepreneur allows you to turn one of your passions into a career. What better way to enjoy life than to get paid for something that you love to do and that deeply motivates you?

PROMOTING MY VALUE

If you truly believe that part of your life mission is to add value to other people's lives, then you need to let as many people as possible know that your knowledge and experience will benefit them. You need to learn how to promote yourself and your value to others with passion and enthusiasm. In your career, how you present yourself to others can mean the difference between advancing or being stuck in a rut. If your present feelings about selling and self-promotion are marked by resentment, rejection or negativity, then you need to take steps to create a more positive attitude about your capabilities and your value to others. All excellent leaders and successful entrepreneurs have learned the skills of presenting their value in a way that is very enticing. Whether you realize it or not, you sell yourself at every meeting you attend, every time you work with others and with every job you do. You have skills and benefits that are valuable to employers. Identifying some of those features is the first step to travelling up the corporate ladder or moving ahead in your career.

Writing an advertisement to sell yourself

On Day One, you identified many of your skills, character traits and talents. In the following exercise, imagine that you are going to write an ad promoting your value to others. Fill in five or six major features you have to offer and the benefits of each.

Feature	Benefit

Now, do your best to write an ad promoting yourself. Use the following example as a template to guide you in the writing process.

Sally Success – a positive, energetic and committed worker. Very few have the drive and motivation that Sally possesses to help others reach their full potential. Her easygoing and sympathetic communication style sets her apart from her peers in putting her clients at ease in order to address their specific needs. Sally is a results and goal-directed consultant who has solid writing and speaking skills. Being a team player she is capable of improving all relationships within any organization. Sally has an extensive background in success coaching that would be a welcome addition to your organization. Sally offers you the solutions for which you are looking.

My advertisement

_____

_____

_____

_____

_____

_____

_____

"Great job!

Give yourself a pat on the back."

FINDING THE RIGHT INVESTMENT PLAN

Step One: Determine what financial freedom means to you.

Not until you take the time to establish what you want out of life now and upon retirement will you be able to develop a plan that will take you there.

What do you see yourself doing in five, ten or fifteen years?

_____
_____
_____
_____
_____
_____

What lifestyle will you be content with having upon retirement?

_____
_____
_____
_____
_____
_____

Step Two: Put together your investment team.

Contact a financial advisor who can advise you on developing your personal plan. You may also want to consult other industry professionals for their perspective, such as successful mentors, lawyers, brokers, bankers, insurance agents or accountants. Try to surround yourself with both brilliant financial mentors and like-minded individuals from your core relationships.

Who could you contact this week to help you get started with your initial plan?

_____

_____

_____

_____

_____

Step Three: Realize that your investment plan comes with a cost.

You may need to delay immediate gratification on items you want right away for the long-term benefits of focusing on your financial future. Giving up comfort and simplifying your life right now, increases your chances of ending up being very comfortable in retirement.

> I found every single successful person I've ever spoken to had a turning point.
>
> The turning point was when they made a clear, specific unequivocal decision that they were not going to live like this anymore; they were going to achieve success. Some people make that decision at 15, some people make it at 50 and most people never make it.
>
> **Brian Tracy**

Step Four: Establish your financial and career goals.

Take a moment to review the ideas and concepts presented in this chapter. Compose a list of eight to nine goals that could possibly be implemented to help reach financial freedom on your journey to total success:

	Possible goals for my finances and career

Review each possible goal and ask yourself these three questions:

- Will this goal align me with my life purpose?
- Will this goal add value to people's lives?
- Will this goal allow me to reach my full potential?

If you are unable to answer yes to any of the three questions, consider setting aside this possibility as a goal right now. Once you have eliminated certain possibilities, take a moment to go back and rank each goal in order of priority from one to nine.

Rewrite your top three choices below.

Example: This month, I will set aside 10% of my paycheck for investment purposes and 10% for charitable donations.

Financial Freedom Goal No. 1: _____

_____

_____

Financial Freedom Goal No. 2: _____

_____

_____

Financial Freedom Goal No. 3: _____

_____

_____

Reflective journaling

Take a few minutes to think about the new concepts that you have learned and what you have learned about yourself. Jot down those thoughts and feelings below.

_____

_____

_____

_____

MY FINANCES & CAREER

CINDY'S SUCCESS TIPS FOR FINANCIAL DEVELOPMENT

As you read each success tip, indicate whether it is:

A. a new idea for me to try

B. an idea I need to research more

C. an idea upon which I need to improve.

_____   Discover the world of stocks and bonds.

_____   Attend a career development workshop or seminar.

_____   Set up a discount broker account for self-directed tax sheltered investments.

_____   Invest in real estate.

_____   Become an entrepreneur. Set up your own part-time or full-time business.

_____   Learn about accounting practices or bookkeeping for your business.

_____   Attend a marketing or sales seminar.

_____   Create multiple streams of income for yourself.

_____   Read a biography about a successful entrepreneur.

_____   Join an investment club or financial education organization.

CINDY'S SUGGESTIONS

These resources may be purchased from your favourite bookstore or online.

The One-Minute Millionaire:
The Enlightened Way to Wealth by Robert Allen and Mark Victor Hansen.
New York: Harmony Books, 2002
www.oneminutemillionaire.com

Secrets of the Millionaire Mind: Mastering the Inner Game of Wealth by T. Harv Eker.
Toronto: HarperCollins, 2005
www.millionairemindbook.com

Rich Dad's Guide to Investing:
What the Rich Invest in, That the Poor and Middle Class Do Not! by Robert Kiyosaki and Sharon L. Lechter. New York: Warner Books, 2000
www.richdad.com

How to Have More Than Enough: A Step-by-Step Guide to Creating Abundance by Dave Ramsey. New York: Penguin Books, 2000
www.daveramsey.com

Day Eight

Piecing it all together

In what specific areas should I focus my energy, time and resources? How do I maintain my focus and monitor my progress over the next six weeks?

We live in a world of countless abundance and incredible opportunities. Now that our North American society has moved out of the Industrial Age and entered the Information Age, access to knowledge is literally at your fingertips with the push of a button. At no other time in history has it been easier for you to be successful and attract unlimited prosperity. Your total success is within easy grasp right now.

Over the past week you have taken the time to learn about yourself and the world around you. Now that you have had a chance to explore each of the key growth areas to total success, your task is to incorporate each of these areas into your personal growth plan. Following your personal growth plan over the next six weeks will develop the positive lifestyle that will support you indefinitely on your total success journey.

At the beginning of this book you made a written commitment to do what it would take to become more successful in your life. Your total success boils down to one simple word—choice. To reach your full potential, continue to honor your written commitment. Focus on making the necessary positive changes to your lifestyle. Any growth plan involves change. It is within your reach to grow to your full potential by embracing change. If you don't change, you are unable to grow, and if you are unable to grow you will not be able to reach your full potential and realize your dreams.

Before you embark on any growth plan, you need to establish where you are at in terms of your specific development in each growth area. Once you have established what you should focus on in order to create a better balance between all six total success areas, you can then select specific goals to both maintain your focus and monitor your progress on a day-to-day basis.

WHERE AM I AT?

One of the most useful tools Cindy and I have found in order to monitor our clients' progress and our own personal progress in each of the six focus areas is a total success balance wheel. If you are a visual learner, it will enable you to get a quick snapshot of where you are at in your personal development and what you need to improve. When a wheel is symmetrical, it rolls along a path with greater ease. When you have balance between your six focus areas, life rolls along with greater ease on your chosen path to total success.

"Success is like a wheel in motion. Successful individuals merrily keep rolling along despite minor delays due to an occasional flat tire or a kink in the rim."

For each of the six focus areas, you will rate your level of satisfaction for personal growth with a number between one and ten. A value of ten indicates extreme satisfaction, whereas a value of one indicates the lowest level of satisfaction.

Base your decision on the following three criteria:

- your own self-awareness of where you are at in your life
- the new knowledge you have gained over the last seven days in each of the focus areas
- any positive feedback you may have received from family members, members of your total success team or possibly a mentor.

Be as honest and open about yourself and your situation as you can be. The objective of this self-analysis is to identify the focus areas that require the greatest growth.

Plot each value on the total success balance wheel as indicated in the example. Many individuals like to add color to their wheels so that the information is easier to see in a visual format. After filling in your wheel, take a moment to reflect on what areas need the largest amount of improvement. Let this tool guide your specific goal selection for your ultimate growth plan.

My total success balance wheel

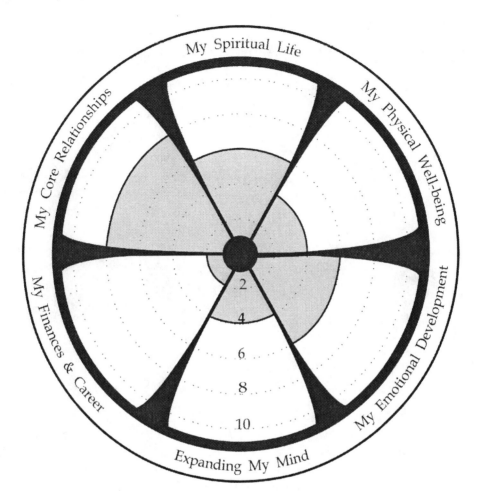

The balance wheel quickly identifies areas in your life that need the focus of your attention. Keep in mind that focusing your attention in one area does not mean that you need to compromise development in the other areas. In other words, you do not need to sacrifice in one area in order to create harmony and balance in all aspects of your life. You will find that within a very short period of time, what you focus your attention on will begin to manifest itself and bring about the necessary change or growth required to achieve total success.

My total success balance wheel   Date: _____

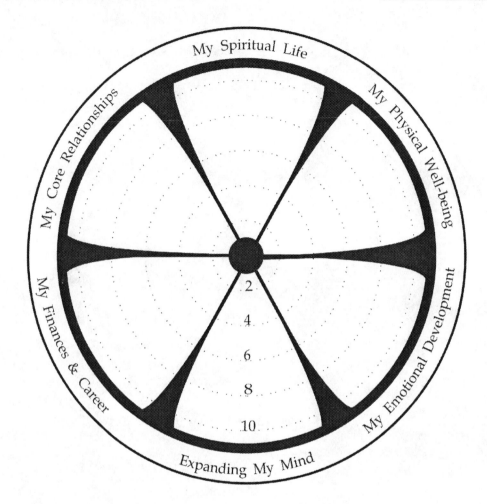

- In which area(s) do I need to spend more time learning and applying the skills and habits that will make me more successful?

- What specific steps could I take to improve those areas that require my immediate attention?

- Which resources and individuals could help me right now with creating better balance between all six key aspects of my life?

- What specific goals do I need to consider at this time in order to create the level of success that I deserve?

Piecing It All Together

SELECTING MY TOP SIX GOALS

Based on the information gleaned from your total success balance wheel, start by choosing one specific goal in each of the total success growth areas that you could focus on over the next six weeks. You may wish to rewrite your top six picks in the space below. Why would you bother rewriting your goals if you already have them in another place? The answer is simple. The more you engage your physical senses in the learning process, and the more you repeat the concepts you would like to focus on or learn in a meaningful context, the easier those concepts or ideas become ingrained in your mind, allowing you to recall the information with greater ease.

	In my spiritual life:
	In my relationships
	In expanding my mind:
	In my physical well-being:
	In my emotional development:
	In my finances and career:

Try to focus on the essentials and nothing more. As the weeks go by and you begin to realize these initial goals, work towards incorporating your other top picks. Do not feel that you need to accomplish every one of your goals over the next six weeks. Allow each goal the time necessary for satisfactory completion.

WHAT ABOUT MY TOTAL SUCCESS TEAM?

The easiest path to total success involves the help of others who are able to guide, support, encourage, motivate and educate you. With this in mind, let us recap what you have already started to explore as possibilities and opportunities that will enable you to reach your full potential and have the greatest impact on those individuals in your life.

On Day Three you established a list of possible candidates for your total success team who could help support your endeavours. If you haven't scheduled a time to start contacting these individuals, now would be the time to do so.

On Day Four we asked you to step outside of your comfort zone and look at connecting to three new sources of information that you do not use on a regular basis. You then identified three individuals from whom you could learn more about these knowledge sources. Over the next few weeks, make a point of expanding your mind and knowledge sources with the help of those individuals who could point you in the right direction for the information you seek.

On Day Six you identified possible contacts you could interview about their success-oriented habits and positive attitude. Have you followed up on that commitment to set up a time to contact them? That individual could be the one contact able to give you the guidance, inspiration and support necessary for growing to your full potential.

On Day Seven you identified someone from your possible success team candidates to help you develop a financial freedom plan. If you have not done so already, take the necessary steps to get your financial affairs in order, which also entails getting some sound financial advice.

Piecing It All Together

ATTRACTING MY FIRST MENTOR

Besides surrounding yourself with your team of supportive growth-minded individuals, ideally, you want at least one of those individuals to be capable of moving you into new and exciting growth opportunities. That is where the role of the mentor comes in.

Mentors are individuals who have a combination of unique talents, experience and knowledge and they are willing to share their expertise.

Mentors can be found in many different areas of personal development such as: spirituality, family relationships, public speaking, fitness, marketing, nutrition or accumulating wealth, to name a few. The opportunities for personal development are endless.

In each of the six areas of development for total success, identify a specific area of expertise that you would like to improve:

My spiritual life: _____

My relationships: _____

Expanding my mind: _____

My physical well-being: _____

My emotional development: _____

My finances and career: _____

Which of the above areas is the one you would most like to improve over the next six weeks?

_____

The next step is to find out who could help you in that endeavour. You may have someone in mind already, know of someone who could help you find an ideal candidate, or you may need to do some research by using the internet, the local Yellow Pages, the newspaper or clubs and organizations.

After you have investigated the names of possible mentors to contact, write at least two candidate's names below:

1. _____

2. _____

3. _____

Identify your top pick. If you feel that you need to, take a moment to write a possible script that you could use in order to make an initial contact with your preferred candidate.

Keep in mind the following points:

- Be sincere throughout your request.
- Get to the point about the nature of your conversation.
- Ask for permission to continue the conversation or to call back at a more convenient time.
- Briefly explain your request in a relaxed tone.
- Ask your closing question, such as: Would you be interested in helping me reach my full potential? or Would you be open to discussing this further?
- Should you get the go-ahead, set up a specific time for your next meeting.

_____

_____

_____

_____

_____

_____

_____

_____

_____

My action plan

Step One: Choose a date and time you will call your prospective mentor. Commit to speaking to him or her in person.

Step Two: Should you get a commitment, follow up with a handwritten thank-you note or card right away. If not, don't be discouraged. Contact the next candidate on your short list.

Step Three: The final step is to create your own strategic plan for achieving total success, once you have done your due diligence in identifying an individual you believe will provide the guidance and advice that will move you ever closer to fulfilling your life mission.

MY MOST POWERFUL ALLY – MY JOURNAL

Many of us are in the habit of keeping some form of journal. Athletes keep training diaries to monitor their progress. Writers use notebooks to jot down insights and ideas. Corporate executives record pertinent information in their agendas. Journaling is a powerful tool to expand your awareness, monitor progress, focus your energy and time, develop positive habits and attitudes, affirm your successes and create optimum balance in your life.

Over the next six weeks, you will use a specific journaling process designed to help you be totally successful. Each activity focuses on what really matters in working towards being successful in each of the six focus areas, as well as developing the positive attitudes and habits that enable you to fulfill your life purpose.

To benefit the most from this specific journaling process, spend about ten minutes every night using the journal. You will have an opportunity to visualize, reflect, review and write during the course of the journaling process. By journaling at the end of your day, you will be able to both celebrate your successes and program your subconscious mind for the next day.

Use the following information to guide you in your journaling.

Today's successes   **Day:** day of the week   **Date:** month/day/year

> It's what you accomplish, not how long it takes,
> that determines your level of success.

Before filling out today's successes, take a moment to read aloud your twelve total success attitudes.

In doing so, your mind is able to focus more readily on your successes.

Then, in point form, list at least one accomplishment, success or job well done for each focus area.

Should you get stuck in one area, make a mental note to focus on that area tomorrow.

This section of your journal allows you to celebrate your daily successes and develop a more positive mindset or attitude.

Reflections: What have you learned or experienced?
Jot down any thoughts or feelings about your progress in realizing your full potential or adding value to others' lives.

Tomorrow's Focus: Indicate how you could have a successful, ten-out-of-ten day tomorrow.

Priorities: List your top three daily goals or priorities for tomorrow. Keep in mind that your choices need to be aligned not only with your daily focus areas, but also with your life mission, personal values and major goals.

Today's successes Day: _____ Date: _____

> It's faith in something and enthusiasm for something that makes life worth living.
> **Oliver Wendell Holmes**

Reflections:

Tomorrow's Focus:

Priorities:

Today's successes   Day: _____ Date: _____

> Don't be afraid to go out on a limb. That's where the fruit is.
>
> **H. Jackson Browne**

Reflections:

Tomorrow's Focus:

Priorities:

Today's successes

Day: _____ **Date:** _____

> It is impossible for a man to learn what he thinks he already knows.
>
> **Epictetus**

Reflections:

Tomorrow's Focus:

Priorities:

Today's successes Day: _____ Date: _____

> We make a living by what we get, but we make a life by what we give.
> **Winston Churchill**

Reflections:

Tomorrow's Focus:

Priorities:

Today's successes   Day: _____ Date: _____

> Take care of your body. It's the only place you have to live.
>
> **Jim Rohn**

_____
_____
_____

_____
_____
_____

_____
_____
_____

_____
_____
_____

_____
_____
_____

_____
_____
_____

Reflections: _____
_____

Tomorrow's Focus: _____
_____

Priorities: _____
_____

SUCCESS IS A FOUR-LETTER WORD

Today's successes   Day: _____ Date: _____

> Money is like manure; it's not worth a thing unless it's spread around encouraging young things to grow.
>
> **Thornton Wilder**

Reflections:

Tomorrow's Focus:

Priorities:

PIECING IT ALL TOGETHER

Today's successes Day: _____ Date: _____

> Without faith, nothing is possible. With it, nothing is impossible.
>
> **Mary McLeod Bethune**

Reflections:

Tomorrow's Focus:

Priorities:

Today's successes   Day: _____ Date: _____

> It's never too late to be who you might have been.
>
> **George Elliot**

Reflections:

Tomorrow's Focus:

Priorities:

Today's successes   Day: _____ Date: _____

> Never worry about numbers. Help one person at a time,
> and always start with the person nearest you.
>
> **Mother Teresa**

Reflections:

Tomorrow's Focus:

Priorities:

Today's successes   Day: _____ Date: _____

> We are drowning in information and starved for knowledge.
>
> **Anonymous**

_____

Reflections: _____

Tomorrow's Focus: _____

Priorities: _____

PIECING IT ALL TOGETHER

Today's successes   **Day:** _____ **Date:** _____

> Luck is a matter of preparation meeting opportunity.
>
> **Oprah Winfrey**

Reflections:

Tomorrow's Focus:

Priorities:

143

Today's successes   Day: _____ Date: _____

> Goals are not only absolutely necessary to motivate us.
> They are essential to really keep us alive.
>
> **Robert H. Schuller**

Reflections:

Tomorrow's Focus:

Priorities:

Today's successes   Day: _____ Date: _____

> It's easy to make a buck. It's a lot tougher to make a difference.
>
> **Tom Brokaw**

Reflections:

Tomorrow's Focus:

Priorities:

SUCCESS IS A FOUR-LETTER WORD

Today's successes   Day: _____ Date: _____

> My success, part of it certainly, is that I have focused in on a few things.
> **— Bill Gates**

Reflections:

Tomorrow's Focus:

Priorities:

Today's successes   Day: _____ Date: _____

> To accomplish great things, we must not only act, but also dream;
> not only plan, but also believe.
>
> **Anatole France**

Reflections:

Tomorrow's Focus:

Priorities:

Today's successes Day: _____ Date: _____

> When people talk, listen completely. Most people never listen.
>
> **Ernest Hemingway**

Reflections:

Tomorrow's Focus:

Priorities:

PIECING IT ALL TOGETHER

Today's successes   **Day:** _____ **Date:** _____

> Knowledge is an antidote to fear.
>
> **Ralph Waldo Emerson**

Reflections:

Tomorrow's Focus:

Priorities:

SUCCESS IS A FOUR-LETTER WORD

Today's successes   Day: _____ Date: _____

> He who enjoys good health is rich, though he knows it not.
>
> **Italian proverb**

Reflections:

Tomorrow's Focus:

Priorities:

Today's successes   Day: _____ Date: _____

> If you aren't making any mistakes, it's a sure sign you're playing it too safe.
>
> **John Maxwell**

Reflections:

Tomorrow's Focus:

Priorities:

Today's successes Day: _____ Date: _____

> The control center of your life is your attitude.
>
> **Anonymous**

Reflections:

Tomorrow's Focus:

Priorities:

PIECING IT ALL TOGETHER

Today's successes　　　　　**Day:** _____ **Date:** _____

> Knowledge becomes power only when we put it into use.
>
> **Anonymous**

Reflections:

Tomorrow's Focus:

Priorities:

153

SUCCESS IS A FOUR-LETTER WORD

Today's successes　　　　　　　Day: _____ Date: _____

> No one has ever become poor by giving.
>
> **Anne Frank**

Reflections:

Tomorrow's Focus:

Priorities:

Today's successes   Day: _____ Date: _____

> The purpose of life is a life of purpose.
>
> **Robert Byrne**

Reflections:

Tomorrow's Focus:

Priorities:

SUCCESS IS A FOUR-LETTER WORD

Today's successes   Day: _____ Date: _____

> Great things are not done by impulse, but by a series of small things brought together.
> **Vincent Van Gogh**

Reflections:

Tomorrow's Focus:

Priorities:

Today's successes   Day: _____ Date: _____

> Minds are like parachutes – they only function when open.
> **Thomas Dewar**

_____
_____
_____
_____
_____
_____
_____
_____
_____
_____
_____
_____

Reflections: _____

Tomorrow's Focus: _____

Priorities: _____

Today's successes   Day: _____ Date: _____

> Prevention is better than cure.
>
> **Desiderius Erasmus**

Reflections: _____

Tomorrow's Focus: _____

Priorities: _____

PIECING IT ALL TOGETHER

Today's successes   Day: _____ Date: _____

> They say that time changes things, but you actually have to change them yourself.
> **Andy Warhol**

Reflections:

Tomorrow's Focus:

Priorities:

Today's successes   Day: _____ Date: _____

> And in the end it's not the years in your life that count. It's the life in your years.
>
> **Abraham Lincoln**

Reflections:

Tomorrow's Focus:

Priorities:

Today's successes   Day: _____ Date: _____

> Your big opportunity may be right where you are now.
>
> **Napoleon Hill**

_____
_____
_____
_____
_____
_____
_____
_____
_____
_____
_____
_____
_____
_____
_____
_____
_____
_____

Reflections: _____
_____

Tomorrow's Focus: _____
_____

Priorities: _____
_____
_____

SUCCESS IS A FOUR-LETTER WORD

Today's successes Day: _____ Date: _____

> Think of giving not as a duty but as a privilege.
>
> **John D. Rockefeller Jr.**

Reflections:

Tomorrow's Focus:

Priorities:

Today's successes   Day: _____ Date: _____

> It is good to have an end to journey toward,
> but it is the journey that matters in the end.
>
> **Ursula K. Leguin**

Reflections:

Tomorrow's Focus:

Priorities:

Today's successes   Day: _____ Date: _____

> A godly life brings huge profits to people who are content with what they have.
>
> **1 Timothy 6:6**

_____

_____

_____

_____

_____

_____

Reflections: _____

Tomorrow's Focus: _____

Priorities: _____

PIECING IT ALL TOGETHER

Today's successes Day: _____ Date: _____

> As one person I cannot change the world, but I can change the world of one person.
>
> **Paul Shane Spear**

Reflections:

Tomorrow's Focus:

Priorities:

Today's successes Day: _____ Date: _____

> Communication leads to community, that is,
> to understanding, intimacy and mutual valuing.
>
> **Rollo May**

Reflections:

Tomorrow's Focus:

Priorities:

PIECING IT ALL TOGETHER

Today's successes　　　　Day: _____ Date: _____

> The key to real health and happiness and success is self-knowledge.
> **Anonymous**

Reflections: _____

Tomorrow's Focus: _____

Priorities: _____

Today's successes   Day: _____ Date: _____

> Those who cannot change their minds cannot change anything.
> **George Bernard Shaw**

Reflections:

Tomorrow's Focus:

Priorities:

PIECING IT ALL TOGETHER

Today's successes   Day: _____ Date: _____

> Knowledge is power, but enthusiasm pulls the switch.
>
> **Ivern Ball**

Reflections:

Tomorrow's Focus:

Priorities:

SUCCESS IS A FOUR-LETTER WORD

Today's successes   Day: _____ Date: _____

> If at first you don't succeed, you're running about average.
>
> **M.H. Alderson**

Reflections:

Tomorrow's Focus:

Priorities:

170

PIECING IT ALL TOGETHER

Today's successes   **Day:** _____ **Date:** _____

> Smile, when picking up the phone. The caller will hear it in your voice.
>
> **Anthony Robbins**

Reflections:

Tomorrow's Focus:

Priorities:

Today's successes   Day: _____ Date: _____

> Many of life's failures are people who did not realize
> how close they were to success when they gave up.
>
> **Thomas Edison**

_____
_____
_____
_____
_____
_____
_____
_____
_____
_____
_____
_____
_____

Reflections: _____
_____

Tomorrow's Focus: _____
_____

Priorities: _____
_____
_____

PIECING IT ALL TOGETHER

Today's successes   Day: _____ Date: _____

> Unless you try to do something beyond what you have already mastered, you will never grow.
>
> **Ronald E. Osborn**

Reflections:

Tomorrow's Focus:

Priorities:

SUCCESS IS A FOUR-LETTER WORD

Today's successes   Day: _____ Date: _____

> In the middle of difficulty lies opportunity.
>
> **Albert Einstein**

Reflections:

Tomorrow's Focus:

Priorities:

Piecing It All Together

WHERE DO I GO FROM HERE?

Congratulations once again. The steps that you have taken over the past fifty days have moved you closer to creating both a successful future and balanced lifestyle. By focusing your time and energy on realizing specific goals in each of the six areas for achieving total success, you have created many positive changes in your life that have enabled you to acquire greater abundance, prosperity and joy. The information you have read, coupled with a call to action, has embarked you on a transformation process that has propelled you along your unique path to total success.

You have taken the hardest step of your journey. By deciding to read this guide, you have taken a major step in your life to rise above the norm and take positive action to reach your full potential. We hope that you have developed a stronger sense of purpose, that you understand what it means to grow to your full potential in all six aspects of having a balanced life and that you are ready to add value to other people's lives. Your challenge now is to continue your efforts. The rewards are worth the commitment of both your time and energy.

Take a moment to fill out another total success wheel to assess where you are right now in your progress, as well as where you might go as you continue your journey. You may also find it helpful to re-evaluate your goals and set a number of short-term goals for the next few months. Setting tangible, achievable short-term goals enables you to stay motivated and on course to realizing more lofty aspirations and dreams.

Continue to make learning an integral part of your daily life. Go back to some of the success tips from each chapter and check out areas that have sparked an interest in further exploration. Please seek out the incredible wealth of knowledge that other success "gurus" have to offer by visiting their websites. You may also wish to access additional tools and resources at our website: www.YourSelfHelpTeam.com.

Both Cindy and I sincerely hope that we have made a significant difference in your life. It is our fervent wish that the concepts and strategies we have presented in this book radically change your life. Please let us know how we may support your future endeavours through our efforts or those of our partner groups. No matter what, keep moving forward to become an even more successful individual than you already are.

My total success balance wheel   Date: _____

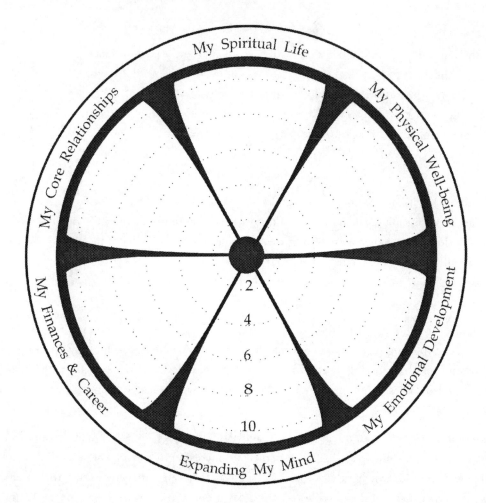

- In which area(s) do I need to spend more time learning and applying the skills and habits that will make me more successful?
- What specific steps could I take to improve those areas that require my immediate attention?
- Which resources and individuals could help me right now with creating better balance between all six key aspects of my life?
- What specific goals do I need to consider at this time in order to create the level of success that I deserve?

ABOUT THE AUTHORS

Randall Stewart

Randall has been involved in both lifestyle and public education consulting for both the Manitoba and British Columbia provincial governments since 1982. In 1988 he founded a language school and communication company in Quebec, which developed and taught tailor-made language courses and communication seminars for private corporations and government agencies. Randall received both his Bachelor of Physical Education and Education degrees from the University of Manitoba. He enjoys competing in cross-country skiing and multi-sport events. Randall's passions include the wine culture, public speaking and mountaineering.

Cindy Stewart

Cindy has worked in the Pacific Northwest in health care and the healing arts since 1979. She holds licences in both nursing and massage therapy. Cindy is also a life coach and health consultant, who enjoys motivating individuals striving to reach their full potential. She loves to both participate and compete in various aerobic sports, such as triathlons, cycling and long distance running. Her passions include the wine and food culture, singing and travel throughout North America.

Both Randall and Cindy live in the Okanagan region of British Columbia where they are active within their church community. A portion of the proceeds from the sale of all of their educational products and services goes towards providing education resources for the less fortunate.

Successful individuals strive to leave both an earthly and eternal legacy founded in unconditional love. They are driven by a desire to learn continuously. Successful individuals have the conviction to live their lives to the fullest, having the ability to laugh and take pleasure in life. Successful entrepreneurs are always looking for opportunities to leverage both their time and financial resources for the betterment of mankind. Both Randall and Cindy would like <u>you</u> to be one of those individuals.

SUCCESS: INTERACTIVE HOME STUDY COURSE

In this inspiring, hands-on, interactive course we walk you through each fundamental area of development for reaching your full potential. Learn the essential skills and specific strategies to create permanent positive change and attract more abundance, prosperity and happiness into your life. Transform your life now! Let this interactive audio CD course be the catalyst to propel you to the next level of your overall success.

(8 audio CDs, workbook and journal)

We have taken much of the guesswork out of what strategies work or are more effective in creating better balance and harmony between all key aspects of your life. The course is divided up into eight concise modules and uses an interactive guide with each audio CD lesson. Your weeklong audio program provides you with the additional benefits not seen in the book:

- greater level of built-in accountability
- engages you in specific step-by-step activities
- provides access to additional tools and resources for your continued growth
- more effectively guides and tracks your progress day-by-day
- organized to optimize your learning time
- re-energizes and motivates you to a greater extent
- verbally encourages you day-by-day
- allows you to delve deeper into each of the six key developmental areas.

This ultimate life mini course is the next best thing to having a one-on-one coach.

Order your program today at www.YourSelfHelpTeam.com.

SUCCESS AUDIO BOOK SUMMARIES

Not enough time to read a lot of self help books? Slash your reading time from hours to just minutes. Each audio book summary presents the key ideas and important insights in just forty minutes, saving you time and money. Learn what the experts are truly saying in a fraction of the time required to read each book. Blitz through some of the best self help books on the market in less time than it takes to read the newspaper. Learn practical tips that you can use immediately. Listen to the top success gurus on the way to work, while working out, or in the comfort of your home.

You get the substance of each book, expertly extracted in a way that preserves the author's spirit and intent. We have taken the guesswork out of which titles deserve your attention and that will make a measurable difference in your life. Listen to experts like:

Dr. Wayne Dyer	Gary Chapman	Robert Kiyosaki
T. Harv Eker	Jack Canfield	Mark Victor Hansen
John Maxwell	John Grey	Gary Smalley
Dave Ramsey	Robert Allen	Steven Covey

Order your first audio collection today at www.YourSelfHelpTeam.com.

Success is a Team Sport. Be a part of our Success Team.

Sign up today to receive our free newsletter and to access other resources and tools to support you on your total success journey.

Visit our site at **www.YourSelfHelpTeam.com**.